The Best
Women's Stage Monologues
# of 2003

Smith and Kraus *Books for Actors*

MONOLOGUE AUDITION SERIES
The Best Men's / Women's Stage Monologues of 2002
The Best Men's / Women's Stage Monologues of 2001
The Best Men's / Women's Stage Monologues of 2000
The Best Men's / Women's Stage Monologues of 1999
The Best Men's / Women's Stage Monologues of 1998
The Best Men's / Women's Stage Monologues of 1997
The Best Men's / Women's Stage Monologues of 1996
The Best Men's / Women's Stage Monologues of 1995
The Best Men's / Women's Stage Monologues of 1994
The Best Men's / Women's Stage Monologues of 1993
The Best Men's / Women's Stage Monologues of 1992
The Best Men's / Women's Stage Monologues of 1991
The Best Men's / Women's Stage Monologues of 1990
One Hundred Men's / Women's Stage Monologues from the 1980s
2 Minutes and Under: Character Monologues for Actors Volumes I and II
Monologues from Contemporary Literature: Volume I
Monologues from Classic Plays 468 BC to 1960 AD
100 Great Monologues from the Renaissance Theatre
100 Great Monologues from the Neo-Classical Theatre
100 Great Monologues from the 19th Century Romantic and Realistic Theatres
The Ultimate Audition Series Volume I: 222 Monologues, 2 Minutes & Under
The Ultimate Audition Series Volume II: 222 Monologues, 2 Minutes & Under
        from Literature

YOUNG ACTOR MONOLOGUE SERIES
Cool Characters for Kids: 71 One-Minute Monologues
Great Scenes and Monologues for Children, Volumes I and II
Great Monologues for Young Actors, Volumes I and II
Short Scenes and Monologues for Middle School Actors
Multicultural Monologues for Young Actors
The Ultimate Audition Series for Middle School Actors Vol.I: 111 One-Minute
        Monologues
The Ultimate Audition Series for Teens Vol. I: 111 One-Minute Monologues
The Ultimate Audition Series for Teens Vol.II: 111 One-Minute Monologues
The Ultimate Audition Series for Teens Vol.III: 111 One-Minute Monologues
The Ultimate Audition Series for Teens Vol.IV: 111 One-Minute Monologues
The Ultimate Audition Series for Teens Vol.V: 111 One-Minute Monologues
        from Shakespeare
Wild and Wacky Characters for Kids: 60 One-Minute Monologues

If you require prepublication information about upcoming Smith and Kraus books, you may receive our semiannual catalogue, free of charge, by sending your name and address to *Smith and Kraus Catalogue, PO Box 127, Lyme, NH 03768. Or call us at (800) 895-4331; fax (603) 643-6431.*

The Best
Women's Stage Monologues
of 2003

edited by D. L. Lepidus

MONOLOGUE AUDITION SERIES

A SMITH AND KRAUS BOOK

Published by Smith and Kraus, Inc.
177 Lyme Road, Hanover, NH 03755
www.SmithKraus.com

© 2004 by Smith and Kraus, Inc.
All rights reserved
Manufactured in the United States of America

First Edition: April 2004
10 9 8 7 6 5 4 3 2 1

Cover illustration by Lisa Goldfinger
Cover design by Julia Hill Gignoux

The Monologue Audition Series
ISSN 1067-134X
ISBN 1-57525-333-X

NOTE: These monologues are intended to be used for audition and class study; permission is not required to use the material for those purposes. However, if there is a paid performance of any of the monologues included in this book, please refer to the Permissions Acknowledgment pages 101–104 to locate the source that can grant permission for public performance.

Contents

Foreword

When Smith and Kraus first asked me to take over their exemplary monologue and scene book series, little did I know what I was getting in for.

I have sifted through hundreds of plays in search of wonderful monologues for actors to use in class or for auditions and then managed, by hook or by crook, to get the rights to print them in this book. Here you will find a wide variety of excellent monologues, for a wide range of performers — though the majority of the pieces I have chosen are for actors under forty as I believe these are the actors with the most pressing need for new monologue material.

Here are fantastic pieces by well-known playwrights such as Don Nigro, Steven Dietz, and Janusz Glowacki, as well as just-as-fantastic monologues by exciting new voices such as Rinne Groff, Brooke Berman, Lisa Soland and Yvette Heyliger.

If you're an actor, or acting student, who prefers to work on material from published, readily available plays, I venture to say that you won't find a monologue book more useful to you than this one. Also recommended: the 2001 and 2002 books, which I also edited.

Thanks to Marisa Smith, Eric Kraus, Julia Gignoux, intern Erin Meanley, and all the agents, publishers and playwrights who allowed me to reprint these wonderful new monologues.

So, actors: You're going out big-game hunting, eh? Well, here are some fine arrows for your quiver. Don't forget to mention Smith and Kraus when you're accepting your Oscar or Tony Award!

— *D. L. Lepidus*

The Anastasia Trials in the Court of Women

Carolyn Gage

Dramatic

Marie/Clara Peuthert (thirties to forties)

> A group of women are staging a trial involving the story of the Grand
> Duchess Anastasia. Five women are put on trial for their failure to
> recognize Anastasia after she escaped the massacre of her family.
> Marie, the bailiff, here is playing a witness.

MARIA/CLARA PEUTHERT: Look, I don't run a hotel. The Grand Duchess
wasn't paying any rent — and she wasn't doing any of the work, either. Picture it: Here she is, the richest Goddamn woman in Europe,
with ten million rubles rotting in some Goddamn account in the
Bank of England, and all she has to do is get the right people to say
she's Anastasia. But does she cooperate? Who's out pounding the
pavement? Clara Peuthert! Who's out talking them into imperial
muck-a-mucks? Clara Peuthert! And if you think it's easy for a woman
who looks like me to walk up to some grand duke and convince him
I'm best friends with the Tsar of Russia's daughter, who I happened
to meet in the lunatic asylum — well, think again. But I did it. I
got them to come see her. And you know what happened? You know
how the Grand Duchess of Russia received her visitors? Like that!
With a Goddamn blanket over her head! And you know what else
she did? She wouldn't speak any Russian. I'm trying to prove she's
the Tsar of Russia's daughter, and she won't say a word of Russian.
German, English, yeah. But Russian? — Nyet! And she knows how
to speak it all right. You should hear her in her sleep. She talks all
night! So how hard can it be to just show a little courtesy, a little
smile, a little *"spasiba"* when someone brings you a present? How hard
is it to take a Goddamn blanket off your head and let them look at

1

you? Is that so Goddamn much for me to ask when I've been slaving my whole Goddamn life away, working fourteen-hour days, killing myself with work for Goddamn near forty years! Is that really so Goddamn much to ask? Hell, yeah, I threw her ass out. And I'd throw it out again!

The Anastasia Trials in The Court of Women

Carolyn Gage

Dramatic

Jenny (twenties to thirties)

> A group of women are staging a trial pertaining to the strange story of
> Anastasia Romanova. Here one of the women lays into the others.

JENNY: Yeah, well, I came here tonight so sick I didn't think I could perform, and none of you gave a Goddamn about that! You — *(To
Marie.)* with your politics *(Marie sits.)* or you — *(To Lisa.)* with your
precious script, or you — *(To Melissa.)* with your critics, or you —
(To Diane.) with your big ideas about changing the world! Nobody
gave a damn about me, so long as I didn't mess up your show. *(To
Athena.)* And then Athena here — my pal — she tricked me into
giving up the lead, so she could have it. But I'm still sick, and I still
lost a lead role and I probably won't draw it again, and making all
of you go sit in those chairs over there isn't going to make me feel
any better or give me back my chance to play the attorney. And if I
tell you all that you're fucked and inhuman and selfish — you know
what? I'm out of a theater company. And Diane is having a hard time
figuring out whether or not Anastasia isn't going to get it anyway,
so who gives a shit? If she'd figured out what the score was in 1922,
she might have made a new life for herself, but it was people like
you — people trying to work off their own guilt — who kept her
trying to be a Grand Duchess for fifty years, when there wasn't even
any imperial Russia anymore. Don't you get it? It's gone. It's over.
The kingdom we had as little girls, that we thought was ours, is fucking gone. It's gone. It went when the babysitter put his hand up our
nightgown, it went when uncle made us suck his candy, it went when
daddy climbed on top of us. It's gone. It's fucking gone and it's never

3

coming back, and all the fucking courtrooms and trials in the world aren't going to bring it back. Never. It's gone. It's fucking gone. It's gone. It's gone. It's gone! *(She begins to choke with rage.)* I don't want your help! I want to be somebody other than a fucking victim before this whole thing's over and it's too late. *(A long pause.)*

Astronaut
M. Kilburg Reedy

Dramatic

Commander Michelle Griffith (late thirties to early forties)

> Commander Griffith, USAF, is addressing the press in a hall at the Kennedy Space Center following a successful pioneering mission to the moon.

COMMANDER GRIFFITH: It's hard to describe. You've seen pictures of the moon, but nothing prepares you for what it's like. The word *desert* isn't enough to describe it, there's nothing like it on Earth. The only color visible is our planet in space, impossibly far away, a swirl of blue and white. The water planet.

You feel so exposed. With no atmosphere, there is nothing to shelter you from the endless space. Nothing to interrupt your view until your eyes reach the horizon and the planet seems to drop off abruptly into emptiness. *(With a smile.)* Not even a Texas prairie mesquite tree, and those damn things can thrive anyplace, on a little sunshine and a helluva lot of nerve. *(Serious again.)* Before I left I spent a day out there with the Land Rover. I was collecting specimens from different rock formations and soil samples from all over the northern hemisphere of the moon. Sealing them into sterile plastic bags. *(Picking up bag of dirt.)* The soil, it was dry. Like powder, ashes. Ancient volcanic rock, pulverized to dust by thousands of years of solar wind and micrometeorites. In some places the dust is thirty feet thick. No moisture, no life. *(Recalling, with some surprise.)* It made me think of my mother. I wanted to smell the dirt in my hands, the way I'd seen her do. *(Sets down the bag.)* When I left, they were just starting to build the first greenhouse. Soil analyses show that moon dirt is tillable. In time, we hope that the lunar colony will be self-supporting, actually capable of producing the food to feed its population. Can you believe that? *(She picks up the bag of dirt again.)* I brought a bag of it back with me. I wish . . . *(Pausing in thought.)* I wish I could take it to her and say, here, Mom. If anyone can do it, you can. Let's see what you can grow with this. *(Lights fade to black.)*

Autobiography of a Homegirl

Yvette Heyliger

Dramatic

Roanetta (early thirties)

Roanetta is an attractive, light-skinned, middle-class, African-American woman, educated and well-bred, who struggles to recoup her self-esteem due to the challenges of living in American society.

Set in 1983, this is a bittersweet play about Roanetta's epiphany when, in a twenty-four-hour stretch, her child's father shows up with his white fiancée, and in an historic coup, the first black women is crowned Miss America.

SCENE: Therapist's office, New York City. Roanetta grapples with the consequences of the life she has chosen (as opposed to the way she was raised) due to the choice she made to have a child and raise that child on her own terms.

ROANETTA: Well . . . I needed to talk to someone. Someone who didn't know me — or all of the associated people involved. I've never been in this position. I don't even know anyone who has been in this position, at least no one who will admit it. You see, I don't come from this. I grew up in a middle-class black family: baby grand piano, oriental carpets, Haitian art, two cars, and cocktail parties, who's who, who ain't who, and who wants to be who. I don't come from this. I went to church. I learned that God was a white man, with a long white beard, peering over a cloud, watching me like a hawk! You can believe he got his fifty cents every Sunday, yes he did! You see I don't come from this.

I went to a private school until the fourth grade. I learned French there from a little French poodle puppet named Fifi. I served toast and tea from strawberry teacups at tea parties for my playmates on rainy afternoons. I was a Girl Scout. *(She raises her right hand, making the Girl Scout sign, as she repeats the "Girl Scout Promise.")* "On my honor, I will try: To do my duty to God and my country, to help other people at all times, to obey the Girl Scout laws . . . A Girl Scout is loyal . . . A Girl Scout is thrifty . . . A Girl Scout is clean in thought, word, and deed. And there are others — ten in all, I think. You see I don't come from this.

I went to Charm School. You know — to learn how to sit, how to stand, how to walk, how to talk, how to eat, the social graces. Ladies don't fart. Did you know that? I never farted. Not once. Honest! I did "poot," however. But I don't think that's the same thing — is it? You see, I don't come from this.

I went to Barbra Streisand movies and to museums on the weekends, or to the ballet. I know every Johnny Mathis album by heart. I saw him in concert once! You know, if you close your eyes, you can't tell the difference between the record and the real thing! Hearing Johnny Mathis live was just like listening to a photograph! It was picture perfect. You see I don't come from this.

I went to boarding school in upstate New York with daughters of owners of big corporations, you know, "old money," and daughters and granddaughters of politicians, girls who had never even been around a black person before. I was a debutante — wore a white dress to my cotillion. I danced the waltz, just like Cinderella — one . . . two . . . three, one . . . two . . . three. I went to college, spent the summer abroad in France. "Bon jour, Mademoiselle!" "Bon jour, Monsieur!" You see, I don't come from this, this WELFARE!

I had no one to talk to, no frame of reference. No one in my family was ever on it. I had no frame of reference. Do you think I like being on welfare? Do you think it's easy for me? Walking through those doors was the hardest thing I ever had to do. Me who writes poetry, who takes art classes, who listens to classical music, who reads the "Arts and Leisure" section of the *New York Times* on Sundays, sipping a mimosa and eating a croissant. Me, the light-skinned, middle-class, bourgeois, spoiled, broken black woman standing on one leg, who wanted to breast-feed. But the hardest part was the fear — fear I would end up like those other welfare mothers, hanging out of windows waiting for the mailman to bring my check, going nowhere, life passing by, baby after baby, different fathers, no books, only TV sets. I mean that's the stereotyped welfare mother, isn't it? You see, I wasn't going to let Craig talk me into throwing my baby in the trash. But, I'm not going to give up my dreams either. I'm in graduate school! Welfare is not *my* career; it's not *my* goal. I'm going to be a professional writer some day. I just need some help right now. That's what welfare's for, isn't it? To help you get on your feet?

I know what you think. You think I should go back home and live with my parents — or be chained nine to five to a secretary's desk with my baby spending its days with someone who is not its mother, no! I want to be there to see baby's first steps, to hear baby's first words, to feel baby's little mouth sucking *my* milk from *my* breasts. Is that wanting my cake and eating it too?

The Beauty Inside
By Catherine Filloux

Dramatic

Latife (late twenties)

> Latife, a city lawyer, decides to defend Yalova, a fourteen-year-old girl, the victim of an attempted honor killing in rural, Southeastern Turkey.

LATIFE: When I was a little girl my own mother died. She died in a car crash — if you ever go to Istanbul you'll see that traffic lights are only there for decoration. They say my mother was the type to stop at them. So . . . I was raised by men. My father, two brothers taught me how to excel, study hard, debate at the dinner table, defend my honor. I went to the best university, was lauded by my teachers, lauded especially by my father and my brothers who always seemed giddy that I, a woman, their creation, succeeded so well, worked out so right. *(With self-deprecation.)* Now I am a senior lawyer, but there is no place to debate at the dinner table about people like you.

Your fate is unthinkable to those who raised me. These men would never understand how in your belly will be your life, yourself, how that woman who walked out the door is still your heroine; how the canal you traveled down is both your road to freedom and the rope to hang you. That silvery mirage you speak of, just out of reach . . . I will fight with what I have been given by those men who honor me so highly. For them it's all for common markets, but that's not what it is for me. I will have to fight this their way, the way my own father taught me, for you, Yalova. Now let me go get the doctor.

Black Thang
Ato Essandoh

Comic

Keisha (black, late twenties to early thirties)

Keisha is recounting her experience with trying to rent a horse-drawn carriage for her wedding. She is talking to her friend and roommate, Mattie, who is white.

Mattie and Keisha's apartment. Keisha is stuffing invitations. Mattie's doing yoga.

KEISHA: So I met the horses last night. Champ and Lucky Lady. You know, to pull my bridal carriage. So now is the time I find out that Omar's grandmother is deadly afraid of horses. Some childhood trauma she had when she was like two when her pet rabbits got trampled to death by a wild stallion. . . .

Yeah, apparently it was pretty bad. Cause there were like 150 baby rabbits in the litter and somehow they got into the stable and the stallion was in heat so it just freaked out — and there were like bloody rabbit ears, and fluffy tails all over the place. And supposedly rabbits make the most awful screeching sound when they're dying. It's supposed to sound like a child crying or something like that. . . .

Yeah. But you would think that after what, seventy-eight years she would have gotten over something like that. Right? I mean come on, she was raised on a farm. She eats fried chicken for Christ sakes. I mean what? Chickens don't make horrible noises when they're getting slaughtered? I bet they do. So they bring out Champ and Lucky Lady, you know, the horses? And my grandmother-in-law-to-be totally freaks out. I mean freaks out. And it was really scary and kinda sad because she's autistic and just had a stroke, so only half of her face works, so it's like a total Dustin Hoffman–*Rainman* kind of freak-out. I mean she starts banging her head screaming "Bunny!" "Bunny!"

11

"Bunny!" which totally freaks out Lucky Lady who proceeds to take the biggest grossest shit I've ever seen right in front of us. I mean ten pounds of shit just drops out of this horse's ass. Just like that. And I'm like: "Is this normal?" And apparently it is? Horses shit without warning! Dogs squat, cats excuse themselves, but horses? No warning just "Sploosh!" Can you imagine if that were to happen during the ceremony? So to hell with the horses I'm renting a limo.

Black Thang

Ato Essandoh

Seriocomic

Mattie (late twenties, early thirties)

Mattie, a white woman, is talking to her friend and roommate Keisha (who is black), about a dream she had about the black man she is dating, whose name is Sam.

Mattie and Keisha's apartment. Keisha is trying on her wedding dress.
MATTIE: OK so there I am on the turnpike. Just me and Mr. Pugglewuck who's driving because it's his turn to drive. And we're driving, flipping through the radio stations. And all of a sudden "Relax" by Frankie Goes to Hollywood comes on! You know that song? *(Singing.)* "Relax! Don't do it! When you wanna sock it to it! Relax! Don't do it when you wanna come! Huh!" I love that song. So does Mr. Pugglewuck and it's so funny because we had just been saying ten minutes earlier how cool it would be if we could hear that song. And there it was! I love when that happens. So anyway it's me and Mr. Pugglewuck and we're driving, and singing and blowing bubbles. Roasting marshmallows in the campfire we've got going in the glove compartment. And we're eating kumquats and Skittles and it's funny because Mr. Pugglewuck who's always been a little on the compulsive side, likes to color coordinate his Skittles before he eats them. So he's got them lined up on the dashboard, you know red, orange, yellow, green, blue, indigo, violet and he's eating them one by one. And that's when I notice that the Skittles are lined up in the exact order of the colors in the visible light spectrum. So I go: "Hey Mr. Pugglewuck! ROY G BIV! Get it?" Which I thought was pretty hysterical but apparently was completely lost on Mr. Pugglewuck cause he kinda just looked at me and blinked. Which, at the time, I thought that was kinda rude. So I was about to say something when I noticed that instead of arms, Mr. Pugglewuck had fins . . . And that's

13

when things started to get a little weird, Mr. Pugglewuck was actually *the* Mr. Pugglewuck. The sea lion my mother bought me when I was three when my parents and I went to Sea World one summer. Mr. Pugglewuck was my most favorite toy, who I lost on the beach when we went down to the Keys a few years later.

And according to my parents I almost drowned trying to swim out to sea in order to find Mr. Pugglewuck who, apparently, I assumed had run away because he was homesick. I was in a coma for three hours. I of course have no recollection of this. But that's not the point. The point is that what I hadn't noticed until after I woke up is that anytime Mr. Pugglewuck spoke . . . it was with Sam's voice. . . .

What do you think that means?

Blue
Charles Randolph-Wright

Seriocomic

Peggy (thirties to forties)

> Peggy, the matriarch of a black family, is warning her son Reuben about a girl he is seeing.

PEGGY: This one just smells of money. This is the kind of coat you wear down Fifth Avenue. It called out my name — "Peggy! Peggy!" And before I knew it, my credit card had leapt out of my purse, and was dancing down the counter. I tried to stop it, I really did, but charge cards have a mind of their own . . . And you should have seen that new salesgirl's face. A Black Woman with an American Express card from Kent, S.C. almost gave her a heart attack. She held up the cheaper coat and said, *(Imitating her.)* "Should I ring this red one up?" And I said, "Should I wring your red neck?"

Oh, yes I did. She picked the wrong person to mess with today! First, she choked on her gum, then laughed a little nervous laugh, then started fanning herself, complaining about how hot it was. Helpful hint — white people often complain about the heat when trying to stop that word *nigger* from jumping out of their mouths — honey, they complain about the heat . . . So I smiled and simply said, "I'll take both." I thought she was going to pass out right then and there. Angel, let's not tell your father about the coats. He doesn't need that information. We'll simply apply my favorite new quote: "You must not lie, unless you must." Isn't that divine? Did your brother go with your father to get the body?

He's out with some tramp, isn't he? I know he's been seeing somebody, and he's hiding her from me. Find out who she is.

Oh, Reuben, don't let these little lowlife Carolina tramps fool you like they've fooled Sam. You see, we Clarks often prepare questionable types next door in the funeral home, that's different. In business we don't discriminate, but in life, we have a choice. Which means I never, ever want to see you bringing somebody common into this house. Lord have mercy, what kind of children would you have? Hair all nappy — *(Looking at her watch.)* Look at the time. I need to change, and pretend to cook. *(Peggy starts to exit, then turns back to Reuben.)* Baby, you must find out who this tramp is. Don't protect your brother. Someone must de-tramp this family. When your mother asks you to do something, you do it, you understand?

Blue
Charles Randolph-Wright

Dramatic

Peggy (thirties to forties)

> Peggy, the matriarch of a black family, is talking to her son, Reuben,
> about his father, her husband, Samuel, an undertaker, and about a
> fling she had years ago with a singer named Blue, who might be
> Reuben's real father.

PEGGY: It was February 1966. We had a big snow that year. And much
like you, I could not handle all these dead people one more second.
Your father and I had been having problems. He couldn't see *me* anymore. He could only see the families and the ministers and the pall-
bearers and the soloists and on and on and everybody but me. And
I couldn't handle the pressure of being Mrs. Samuel Clark. So we
decided to separate for a while. But the Clarks don't fail at anything,
so it was a mandate that I told no one we were separating, and I went
back to Chicago. Everyone here was told that my mother was ill. I
tried to get my life back, but I wasn't the Fashion Fair model any
longer. I was a failed wife, and a mother with a four-year-old. And
one night I met Blue, and *he* saw me. I wasn't a failure. I was a model
again. I was beautiful. Blue was gone on one of his tours, and Samuel
called me, and asked me to come home. I missed Samuel, and I realized that I really did love him because Samuel actually treated me as
his partner, something Blue could never do. Samuel did see me — as
his equal. I had to go away to see that. Blue was only a sound on a
record. Samuel was something I could hold onto. So I came back
home. I didn't know I was pregnant . . . You have to say something.
You can't just sit there. When I found out I was pregnant, I was dis-
traught. I wanted to die. Samuel simply said, "He'll be my son. I
want no one ever to know." Samuel used to drive me insane with
how easily he dealt with things. He doesn't like drama, and I thrive

on it. Things don't seem worth it when you don't fight for them. But when that nurse put you in my arms, and you looked at me, I knew everything would be divine, because you were divine. We brought you home, and you became a Clark. But I was also determined to teach you about your real father. That's why I told you everything I knew about him and his music. And Samuel let me do that. He let me do that. He loved you that much.

Your father could not have been "the" Samuel Clark if we had told anybody the truth . . . One day, and I hope it's not too far away, because I couldn't bear it, you will forgive me. I won't ask you to understand. I just ask you to forgive me.

Boiling People in My Coffee

Jonathan Yukich

Seriocomic

Dorian (forties to fifties)

> CONTEXT: Still mourning the death of her son, whose corpse remains on the living room couch, Dorian speaks with her husband about imaginary people in her morning coffee.

DORIAN: Sometimes I think there are boiling people in my coffee. I know it's odd, but, I tell you, I wonder. Small persons, tiny beings . . . in my coffee. Invisible to the eye, they are. Invisible to all the major senses. Very small, these people. Very, very small. Small brains, small hearts, small toes. Like Swift's Liliputians, except smaller. Itty-bitty. Total size equals a tenth of an atom. A mere tenth, Donald. A single tick-tack would crush millions. Shrimp would consume entire villages in massive gulps. Ants would use them as bowling balls. We're talking small, Donald. These are not big people. They are micro-people. Yes, micro-people . . . in my coffee. Boiling. *(Speaking to her coffee.)* Hello, micro-people! I know you're there! Don't speak. Conserve your energy. I realize you must be in a great deal of pain at the moment. After all, you *are* boiling. I must apologize. You're so tiny that I didn't notice your micro-community in my coffeepot. Therefore, naturally, I filled it with water and let it heat. You're so weak that I didn't hear your tiny screams, so small that I couldn't see your S.O.S. If I had, you may rest assured, I would have stopped. Certainly, I would have stopped. Donald could do without his coffee for a day while you relocated, but I had no idea, you see. None at all. Until now. Oh, the agony you must be going through. I'll drink no more. I'm sorry for the friends and family I've already consumed, but I'll drink no more. No more! A ban on coffee in this household!

I hereby disclaim all coffee in this household! *(To Donald.)* Hanging tideless in our boiling coffee, our micro-people plead for a sympathetic superior. Will you show mercy, Donald, or will you vanish them with vengeance? Will you put your mug down and grant them liberty or will you sip their civilization into oblivion like the arrogant ass face that you are? Will you assert your obligation to them or do you even care? Will you climb higher and higher, mightier and mightier, bathing with indifference? Or will you assert your obligation? Do you even know your obligation, Donald? Oh, please say you do! *(Donald nods.)* Then assert it! Sense their piercing cries, heard only by the coffee dolphins! Sense their melting hearts, beating with heated anguish, longing for a coffee cruise ship! Ever hopeful, they are, until their last merciful gasp! Assert your obligation, Donald! Confirm their faith! Hear their screams! "By the power of God," they call, "By the power of God!" They plead for your obligation! "By the power of God! By the power of God! By the power of God!" Save them! You're obligated, Donald! By the power of God, save them!

The Bridegroom of Blowing Rock

Catherine Trieschmann

Dramatic

Elsa (forties)

> This drama takes place in a rural community in North Carolina in 1865. Here Elsa, the family's matriarch, describes a run-in she had with some Union soldiers.

ELSA: They ain't said a word but pushed me from the door to the floor. They looking for something to eat, they say. Say they calling on behalf of the Union government, that Abraham Lincoln hisself said we oughta be taking care of their needs. One of 'em sticks his foot up my skirt, and that's when Jeremiah got mad. He ain't never stood for nobody to put claim on what's his, so he grabs me up, says there ain't nothing in the house for them and either they leave or he'll shoot them out the door. They all laugh mighty hard at that, and whilst one of 'em holds me down, the other two take out a rope, tie a noose 'round Jeremiah's neck, and string him up high on the beam running down the center of the house. That rope ain't pulled tight enough to kill Jeremiah, but they leave him hanging there 'til his face turns blue, kicking him, cussing him. Soon as I think he's sure as dead, they cut him down. Say they want to know if'n he's ready to tell them what they want to hear. I tell 'em straight, there's chickens in the barn they can eat raw for all I care, but it's high nigh time for 'em to leave me and boy in peace. Reckon their hunger got the better of their meanness, 'cause they all left for the barn, leaving Jeremiah and me on the floor. Then Jeremiah whispers Laurel's name, and I remember I sent Laurel to the barn for eggs. So being as there ain't no choice, I take Jeremiah's musket from my quilt trunk, aim out the front window and shoot one of them three men dead square in the back. I'm reloading when the other two come through the door. The first takes no pause, jest rams his musket blade through Jeremiah's heart. The second takes the musket from me and hits me 'cross the face. Don't know why he ain't kilt me. I wish he had.

Cabo San Lucas
Lisa Soland

Dramatic

Grace (thirties)

Grace was abandoned by a fiancé as they were about to leave for a
Cabo San Lucas honeymoon. After taking an overdose of sleeping
pills, her house is burgled by two incompetents. By this point in the
play, the pills are really beginning to take effect. Guy, the remaining
robber, is on the phone trying to call an ambulance for Grace.

GRACE: *(Grace finds the gun in the couch and holds it on Guy, almost steady.)*
Put down the phone. You're not calling anyone. You've got your whole
life in front of you. Those were the words you were trying to say to me
earlier but you couldn't, but it's true for you, Guy. You really do.
(Beat.) And it's obvious you have no criminal experience prior to this
evening . . . so I'm not going to let you throw away your future just
because I have none. I've made my choice. *(She crosses to left arm of couch
and sits. Her words are beginning to slur.)* I know — "Suicide is a per-
manent solution to a temporary problem." But that's where they're
wrong. My problem is not a temporary one, you see? This has been
going on for a very long time. I have always felt alone my entire life.
If the world was different somehow, slower maybe . . . Jeez, I don't know.
(Finding the right words, with strength.) If people could see someone who
isn't like them. *(Beat.)* Well, anyway, that's why I can do this. I'm an
exception. *(Beat.)* And I don't think I know more than God. In fact, I
know I don't because I have no earthly clue why He would create such
a world — a world like this. *(Lifting the gun back up, she holds it steady
on Guy once more, continuing to press her point.)* Listen, I am one, tiny
little puzzle piece in this world. I don't pretend to know all the pieces
but I know mine. My piece. And if I was meant to "be" then I would-
n't be able to do it, right? To end it. That's what I figure, I mean, if by
God, we were not allowed to take our own life, then it would be im-
possible for me to do so. Am I right?

23

Cabo San Lucas
Lisa Soland

Dramatic

Grace (thirties)

> Grace was abandoned by a fiancé as they were about to leave for a
> Cabo San Lucas honeymoon. After taking an overdose of sleeping
> pills, her house is burgled by two incompetents. By this point in the
> play, the pills are beginning to take effect. Guy, the remaining rob-
> ber, has just asked Grace why she's "through with this living thing."

GRACE: I'm tired. Tired of everything. *(Continuing.)* Taking a shower,
brushing my teeth, eating. Facing the day. Everyday things. I'm so
freakin' tired of them. They do nothing but remind me that I'm by
myself. *(Beat.)* I mean, I've been alone my whole . . . pretty much,
my life. But it got harder as I got older. I watched all my friends get
married and have children and their lives just get so busy. Have you
no idea how busy everyone is? So busy. The whole world. Buzzing,
buzzing, buzzing. And they have to let you know how busy they are.
(Calling out to Guy.) Have you ever noticed that? They have to let
you know how busy they are so it really sinks in how truly insignif-
icant you are to them and it's just because you've set different priorities than them. Priorities like sitting and talking and listening and
doing nothing . . . nothing but being with each other. But heck, your
priorities don't matter because there's no one really to do your priorities with, but yourself, because everyone else is so . . . buzzing.
No one really sees each other any more. *(She responds to the cold
and continues to explain.)* No one really sees you! No one even really
looks. No one has time to look. And even if they do? Even if by some
strange accident, yours and another person's eyes meet in this busy world
. . . they still don't really see you. Take you in. Not really. *(Looking
out.)* I see them. I see them and I see the pain. And I see them not
being able to see me. *(Very vulnerable.)* It's like I'm not even here.

Though I feel so . . . here. It gets confusing. *(Beat.)* I wanted to go to Niagara Falls for our honeymoon. Niagara Falls. *(Growing deeper in her sorrow.)* But he said it's trashed now. It's not like it used to be in the fifties, when people married for life. "For life." *(Stumbling, she makes her way to photo of her with ex-fiance and the fake water-fall.)* That's what he said, "For life," and it ended between the pro-posal and the marriage vows. Could you ever do such a thing to a person?! *(She sits on small table Stage Right, to steady herself.)* People ask about it, why it ended, and I don't know what to say to them? How to explain? *(Becoming upset.)* And even if I do, they don't hear my answer. They don't hear what I say to them. They only hear what would have happened if it was happening to them, in their life. But not to me. Not me in my life. Their life. You see? *(She stands with photo and looks into it as if it were a mirror.)* I'm just a reflection of them in their lives. I don't exist. They don't hear me, Guy, and I don't exist.

Chain Mail
Frederick Stroppel

Seriocomic

Danielle (twenties to thirties)

> Danielle is trying to calm down her husband, Nicky, who has become obsessed to the point of paranoia about his mail.

DANIELLE: Have you been sitting here all afternoon brooding about this? And you didn't go back to work?

Nicky — it's only a *letter.*

Did you at least call in? Nicky, you have a job, you have a responsibility to let them know if you're not going to be there.

I'm worried about you. You know, you're really starting to upset me.

Look, I know how this can happen. You get into a mood, some small thing sets you off, you can't deal with it — it's happened to me. Remember the other day, I wanted to shave my legs, and I couldn't get the package of disposable razors open, and I just *freaked* — remember? I was a basket case. And what did you say? "It's no big deal." And it *was* no big deal, you were right. So let's look at this logically. There's nothing official about this letter. It's not from the I.R.S., it's not from the draft board, not jury duty . . . Not certified, there's no proof that you received it. So there's no penalty for opening it. What could it possibly be? Maybe it's an invitation. Maybe it's a surprise — a *good* surprise. Or maybe it's junk mail, and they didn't put a return address because they were afraid you wouldn't open it. Or maybe it's X-rated material, something we can laugh at. Whatever it is, it's just a letter. It's just a piece of paper. It can't hurt you.

Look, it's not completely anonymous — there *is* a postmark. "Rochester, New York." There you go.

How can it be a fake?

Don't you have a cousin who lives outside Rochester?

Chronicles

Don Nigro

Seriocomic

Dorothy (twenty-four)

> Dorothy Armitage, age twenty-four, speaks to us from the Gothic old Pendragon house in east Ohio near Christmas in the year 1920. Dorothy had a fever when she was a child, and now can't hear anything or speak clearly to the others in the play, but we, the audience, have the privilege of sharing the perfectly clear monologue narration that runs in her head as she leads us through this play. She is funny and stubborn and everybody loves her, and because people tend to forget that she's around sometimes, she knows a lot. The family has gathered from various places for Christmas, in part because Dorothy's father Matthew Armitage is dying. The people she speaks of here are her step-brother Davey Armitage, a poet with a tragic love life; her sister Lizzy, who cooks and cleans with a passion to hide her grief at the loss of her child, and who bosses Dorothy around a lot; their clumsy younger sister Molly, who is a disaster in the kitchen; her parents, who are estranged for reasons Dorothy can't understand; her uncle Rhys, whose return to the house has precipitated a crisis; and her younger sister Jessie, a beautiful bundle of energy that Dorothy just adores; and the housekeeper Sarah, who keeps the family together and is perhaps the only sane person in the house. Dorothy is trying to understand her family by telling us about them.

DOROTHY: Isn't Davey a sweetheart? He's very sad, though. I know he's a poet, and poets are supposed to be kind of melancholy, but sometimes I wish he was more shallow so he could be happier. It's about that woman he was in love with, that dancer. I don't know the details. Everything around here is a little mysterious. I suppose I better get in the kitchen before Sarah and Lizzy kill Molly. That wouldn't be the first person murdered in this house, to hear stories. But which stories are true, and which aren't, is hard to say. Father and Mother are not deeply into reminiscing. If there ever was a time to sort all this messy history out, it'd be now, because everybody still alive is here for once, except for Rhys. I have this fragile set of memories of Rhys being here when I was a very small girl — that would have been around 1901, when Molly was just a baby, and Jessie wasn't born yet. What's wrong between Father and Mother has something to do with Rhys, but I'm not sure what. There's layers and layers, as the boy said looking in the chicken coop. I wish there was some children around so I'd have somebody to talk to. Maybe I can coax the cat out from behind the ice box. The cat is the only sensible person in this house, and Molly goes and pours pudding all over him. I don't know. When I try to think back to what happened when Rhys was here, it's all blurry, like rain on dirty windows. The sounds are in my head, but they're all twisted up with the pictures. Well, here I go. If I'm not back in an hour, you'll know Molly accidentally brained me with the butter churn. That girl needs help.

The Circus Animals' Desertion

Don Nigro

Comic

Becky (eighteen)

Becky Armitage, age eighteen, is in her slip. She getting ready to go out to the carnival one October evening in 1945, in the upstairs room at her Aunt Moll's house where she lives with her two little girls, both the illegitimate children of a traveling carnival man Romeo DeFlores, who keeps impregnating her in the house of mirrors and then leaving town. But Becky is haunted by the ghost of her dead husband, Albert, the town librarian, who married her to give her children a father, but who went mad and hung himself in the barn when he realized she was still going to the carnival to meet Romeo. Becky is a pretty and charming but lost girl whose mother Jessie died when she was born. She doesn't mean to hurt anybody, but her nervous and rather scatterbrained approach to life gets her and the people who love her into trouble a lot. She's singing a forties swing tune that she seems to be making up as she goes along, when Albert's ghost appears.

October 1945. Evening. Becky in her slip, getting ready to go out.
BECKY: *(Singing absently to herself a forties swing tune, not very recognizable.)* Boogie woogie. Boogie woogie. Boogie woogie. Doodliop do me on the jive, Clive. Doodliop do me on the woo woo. *(She is doing her lipstick in the mirror. Albert appears behind her. He is dead, rumpled, pale, and a bit greenish, but looks otherwise much as he did in life.)* Woo woo woo. Doodliop do me on the woooo woo. Doo doo. Doodliop do me on the — *(She sees him in the mirror.)* AHHHH-HHHHHHH. *(She jumps, falling off her stool and smearing lipstick across her face.)* Will you stop doing that? I mean it, Albert. You've

got to stop sneaking up on me like that. You're not dead. Well, OK, you're dead, but you're not here. Well, you're here, but not really. See what you did? I look like Old Weird Bertha who lives at the dump and has a pet rat. *(She begins wiping off lipstick and repairing her makeup.)* Don't talk to me.

You're not sorry. You like scaring me. Why am I even talking to you? I am not going to be crazy, Albert, do you understand? I am not going to be a crazy person. I'm going to be perfectly normal, or as near to that as I can fake, and I'm not going to waste my time talking to my dead husband any more. Christ, I used to make fun of you for talking to yourself all the time, and now I'm doing it, only what's worse is, I'm talking to myself and there's somebody here, and he's dead.

The babies spent the day with Aunt Liz. They've been driving me berserk. Lorry screams and throws things all the time. She throws her food at me, she throws alphabet blocks at me, and when I change her diaper she throws shit at me. And June is all over the place now, and she's so weird. I mean, she's not exactly bad, she just — does bizarre things. She keeps trying to crawl out the window, and this is the second floor, and she hides in her closet and I have to go looking for her. The other day I had the window open and I walked in here and she had a bird on her head. A little bird, it was a wren or something, sitting right on top of her head, and June was just looking at it in the mirror and saying "Birdy, birdy." Weird. And Uncle Clete is driving me crazy with his dumb jokes and his welding in the garage and slapping me on my butt in the kitchen, and if I hear "The Star Spangled Banner" played one more time on the tuba, I swear, I'm going down there and stuff that instrument up Billy's rectum. And I keep seeing my dead husband every place. Other than that, things are just peachy.

Coelacanth
Frederick Stroppel

Dramatic

Frances (thirty-one)

> Frances has taken her brother, Lee, on a whale-watching boat. Here
> she is talking to someone else on the boat (unseen), about her brother,
> who is retarded.

FRANCES: He loves *Mary Poppins*. The little dancing penguins? He imi-
tates them. He can imitate anything. He's got a talent. So it's funny
how things turn out. You think you're going to be one thing, you
turn out to be another. I went into teaching, I don't know what happened. You just never know. I remember when Lee was born, he was
the most beautiful baby — he's still beautiful . . . He's mad at me
now. Are you mad at me? *(Lee doesn't answer.)* Well, he was the most
beautiful child. He had this glow about him, he made you think he
was going to do something remarkable when he grew up. Just gave
you that feeling. Of course, as it turned out . . . What happened,
when he was five years old, we were over at my aunt's house, and he
jumped into an empty pool. He didn't fall, he actually jumped. And
landed on the side of his head. Crazy thing to do. *(To Lee.)* Why did
you do that, you silly? *(Aside.)* He was unconscious for half an hour,
and then they put him in the hospital. And he was never right after
that. Never right. Although, personally, I don't — *(Lowers her voice.)*
I don't think that's what caused it. I think that's why he jumped in
the first place, because there was *always* something not right about
him. Just my theory, but it makes sense. Because you read about most
people, when they get hit on the head, it knocks something loose,
they start killing people. That's how you get serial killers. And he's
not a serial killer. He's just my little brother. *(Beat.)* But he's all right
now. Things are stable. It was a little rocky when my Mom died. They

31

were very close. He lived in that house all his life. But we had to sell it to pay more bills, so he's living with us, my husband and me, for the time being. It's working out fine. Eventually he'll get his own place. That's the most healthy thing. Right, Lee?

Coelacanth
Frederick Stroppel

Dramatic

Frances (thirty-one)

> Frances has taken her brother, Lee, on a whale-watching boat. Here
> she is talking to someone else on the boat (unseen), about her brother,
> who is retarded.

FRANCES: *(Fondly.)* Look at him. Popeye the Sailorman. He's so happy.
He's a happy person. For years I kept thinking that the real Lee was
buried somewhere inside, that someday he'd come out — you know,
like a groundhog — or that maybe we could somehow reach through
to him. But with time you come to realize, this *is* the real Lee. No
one's trapped inside, screaming to get out. He's right there, that's him.
Perfectly happy. *(Sighs.)* It makes you wonder, doesn't it? Some people have everything, all the breaks in the world, and he has so little.
I mean, not that *I've* had everything. Not that my life has been a box
of Lucky Charms . . . But it makes you wonder.

　　He can drive you crazy. I worry what's going to happen to him.
He's so sweet, so trusting, and God knows, this isn't the world for
that kind of attitude. I just wish he could stay with us forever, but
that wouldn't work. I mean, Ray — my husband — he's good, he
makes allowances, but he has a limited amount of patience. And I
don't blame him, it's not what he bargained for. It's not what any of
us bargained for. It tears me up inside — everything he's been
through . . . People can be cruel. Kids. Kids can be fucking cruel.
When he was just a boy, they would throw rocks at him, and say the
most disgusting things . . . No compassion at all. Once he had an
accident in his pants, and they started calling him "Leak" instead of
Lee. Then it was Leak the Freak, Leak the Geek . . . The Missing Leak.
I tell you, every time I hear someone talk about the innocence of children . . . *(Laughs.)* Of course, the thing is, he doesn't even remember

those things. Honestly, he doesn't. I'm the one who has to re-member. I have these horrific memories, and he's just over there, watching the clouds . . . People don't realize, the real hardship is on the family. He doesn't know what he's missing. I do, I know the life he could have had. I'm the one who suffers. You see how I have to clean up for him, get him his food . . . help him get dressed. He can dress himself, but the clothes he picks . . . ! So who's going to take care of him if I'm not around? We used to hope he'd maybe get a girlfriend, someone he could be with . . . There was this one girl at the church where we go, he had a little crush on her, used to fol-low her around, and she was very sweet and understanding, a lovely person, really, but of course, she couldn't, there was no . . . And it almost got to be a problem. We had to keep him home for a while. Let's face it, you're not going to find someone normal for him . . .

Concertina's Rainbow

Glyn O'Malley

Dramatic

Maureen (forty-one)

> This is a direct address to the audience. Maureen is starting to feel her age.

MAUREEN: *(To the audience; ebulliently at the top; confidential.)* All right! There was a lot of sex. Between the "Day of His Walking Out," and, well . . . *(She winces.)* . . . a few months ago. I don't mean just with anyone, but I don't mean with the same man either. If sex is power, then you could say my turbines were spinning at a pretty . . . high . . . voltage. *(Slight pause.)* You run into the arms of men. Your last "hurrahs!" You're forty-one and still can do! You work up a jolly sweat that dries as you head out the door. In the mirror, painting your eyes, you blink amazed, and pleased at how un-needy you are. Finally, you've learned something after all you've been through. But, no. One day in the shower you watch a rivulet pool in a crease you can't remember being there. Drying your hair, you notice the inside of your arm . . . jiggle . . . loosely . . . and you think of lilies wilting on their stalks. You drop your towel, and race sopping wet into your bedroom, your living room, the alcove where the table sits. You snatch the bouquets you've bought for yourself out of every vase. Over the garbage disposal, as it chews them to pieces, you realize that you weren't prepared for how blatantly cold . . . not just life, but . . . you . . . have become. Then . . . void; darkness, like this . . . *(She indicates the shadows at the edge of the light.)* . . . on the other side of the kitchen window, and in the house as the night settles down, and you don't flick a switch on. You don't go on your hot date of the moment . . . *(We hear a telephone ring.)* You don't answer the ringing telephone. You do nothing, but let it come. You haven't moved from your silent, stainless steel sink. You wait for your reflection in the window to comfort you, but it doesn't come. You speak to yourself, or . . . whomever . . . because you want to believe that there is something more than just you rattling in your head. You . . . yearn — which I guess is a prayer — that some . . . inner light will flare up, that you'll see who's reflected back with a new . . . clarity. But no "inner light" . . . comes. You stand there: hair a dried mop; paralyzed; lines, deepening between the absence out there beyond the kitchen window of your new Co-op overlooking the back scruff of Florida, and . . . you.

Concertina's Rainbow
Glyn O'Malley

Dramatic

Maureen (forty-one)

This is a direct address to the audience. Maureen is starting to feel her age.

MAUREEN: *(To the audience.)* Not very often, maybe with a job or . . . or . . . marriage . . . you feel you are ascending; life is pushing you forward and you know there's no going back. You say "Yes!" instead of all the gnawing nos you're used to blurting out with one well-oiled qualification after another. Instead, you say, "Yes!" before you realize the word has flown from your mouth! Then the world is racing past your two wide-open eyes while the "committee" in your head convenes, and the gavels pound and the "don'ts" get shriller and shriller! But "Yes!" has bugled out of you. Your own steam has trumpeted that single monosyllabic from your lungs, and your heart right there between them is booming! And it's the first time in years you've ever felt it pound like that! The first time in years you knew it was the center of your engine! The first time in years you've felt so alive! You don't care because you *do* care so much. "Yes" takes you to the airport. "Yes" takes you on a plane. "Yes" takes you into Economy because Business Class is sold out and you have to be there! *(She buckles herself into her seat.)* "Yes" is right there in the click of your seat belt — the engines whine, the Earth does move and the ascent you feel inside is happening! And . . . and . . . and . . . oh dear God in heaven hold my hand . . . YES!

Doppelganger
Jo J. Adamson

Seriocomic

Young Woman: a passenger on a cruise ship, twenties.

> When the ship's photographer offers to take her picture, the young woman ruminates on her appearance.

YOUNG WOMAN: A thousand things go through my head as the photographer checks the light. Is my lipstick glossy? Cheeks luminous?

Figure voluptuous. Eyes bright, teeth pearly? Hair, curly? Will I project the correct image?

Young woman vacationing? Young Miss Contemplating? Ingenue Visits Atlanta. Society Deb. On Verandah. Young Beauty Soaks Up Sun. American Miss Visits Venice. Austrian Lass Studies Sunset. Fraulein Heinler Smiles at Photographer. Mademoiselle Cline Boards Luxury Liner.

Focus your lens on my tight skin
I was born for the close-up
The sun is my friend: I open like a flower
Count compliments that blossom in the
Summer of my hours

Come to me. Come *on*. Photograph the light around my cells. The shadow of my smile. Soft focus me to the edge of eternity. I'm the infinite closing of your iris shot. The particle in your eye that won't wash out.

Feel me to the whorls of your fingers
Preserve the dream emulsion in your soul
Embalm the Celluloid daylights out of me and

"Oh, please don't die, Beast," Beauty said. "I promise never to leave you again. I'll do anything to save you."

"Will you marry me, Beauty?" asked the Beast.

What do you think, Heather? Should she say yes? Beauty is the only one who can break the spell. She's the only one who can see past his horrible, Beastly exterior to the hurt little boy inside. She's the only one who can heal his wounds and make him happy.

You really think she should? But what if he doesn't turn into a Prince? What if she marries him and he's still the same old Beast, day after day for the rest of their lives?

What do you think happens in the story? That's right.

Beauty kisses the Frog, and he turns into a Prince. Wait a minute, that's not the same story. On second thought, yes it is. Beauty swallows her misgivings and kisses the Frog/Beast, and the next thing you know he's bringing her flowers, and telling her he loves her in eight different languages, and calling her when he says he's going to call, and asking her how her day went.

The next thing you know, he's actually listening to her for a change, and he really seems to care what's on her mind. Pretty soon relaxed, and having a wonderful time. He laughs at her jokes. doesn't have the horrible anxious feeling that if she pauses for a to collect her thoughts, he'll jump in and change the sub-

ally she starts to feel a little guilty because she's talking so d she says to him, "So how are *you*? Tell me how *you* are." ys... *(She laughs, unbelievingly.)* ... he says, "Oh, that's nt right now. Go on with your story." *(Sadly; to Heather.)* that for a fairy tale?

I'll look good in tomorrow's photogravure.
(Young Woman assumes different poses.)

How do you want me?
It's a rhetorical question.
Fetching? Perhaps
Whimsical, capricious, coquettish to be sure
Here's Pert, Saucy, Bewitching . . . Alluring

I give you, Tantalizing, Teasing, Tempting, always.
I am by instinct.
Toss of head, angle of chin, curve of neck
Always right
Up to the orgasmic dissolve

We work well together
Where do you stop and I begin?
I await your separation
In safe-light suspension
O.K., I'm ready
Click the shutter

(Young woman becomes flustered, unsure.)

I'm all aflutter
You'd think I'd be used to this
Each time is like the first virgin thrust
One more minute,
My makeup's running, nose shiny . . .
No! I'm beauty's perfection
The stuff dreams are made of

"No sweat" as they say,
Click the shutter while the feeling rises
Take the wave at its crest

Now! Fire when ready, Sir
I'm at my best

Etta Jenks
Marlane Gomard Meyer

Dramatic

Etta (early thirties)

Etta has come to Hollywood in hopes of becoming a star, but she has found that it is not as easy as she had thought. Here, she is talking to her boyfriend, Burt.

ETTA: I think my throat is closing up. Those French fries were so dry. I think they're caught . . . like a lump in my throat. I think those fries got caught in my throat. I wish I had a Coke. I saw this science experiment once, where they put this tooth in Coke, and over a period of a few weeks or days . . . or maybe it was just one day, it completely fell apart. Just disappeared. I guess that could happen with a whole set of teeth if we were to sit around with a mouthful of Coca-Cola day and night. I wonder how it would work, the teeth comin' out, would you swallow and then what, would they come back in . . . somehow? God, I'm stupid. What am I supposed to do? I thought by now I'd at least have some kinda extra work, somethin' . . . I met this girl, Sheir, at the lunch counter? I thought she was pretty weird but she came out to be nice and she said that one way to break into movies is to have a videotape of yourself made. Performing a scene with someone or maybe doin' a monologue. But the problem is, it costs. I wonder how I could get five hundred dollars? I had four hundred, but that's just about gone. I wonder if I could find somebody with one of those video cameras you use at home? *(She nudges Burt, he looks at her.)* Do you know anybody with a . . . home movie camera?

Fairy Tale Romance
M. Kilburg Reedy

Seriocomic

Woman (thirties)

The speaker is in the midst of reading a bedtime story to [her ...] old daughter.

WOMAN: Oh, don't say that Heather. He's not a jerk. W[...] is right, it's not very grown-up to pout, but he [...] cause he's afraid of getting hurt. He doesn't m[...] a curse his wicked stepmother put on him, a[...] women. But if Beauty loves him enough, h[...] then he won't be a Beast anymore, because[...] leave him.

The Beast gave Beauty a ring, a[...] finger when you go to sleep tonigh[...] you decide to return, pull it off yo[...] returned to my palace."

When Beauty awoke the [...] at home. She was overjoyed [...] the week was up, but Bea[...] Every day she said to her [...] evening she said, "Just [...]

Then one night [...] garden that she kn[...] pulled the ring o[...] morning, she w[...]

Beauty w[...] for the Beas[...] she found [...]

"Ah [...]

cause you [...]

42

The Fourth Sister
Janusz Glowacki

Comic

Tania (twenties)

This dark comedy takes place in contemporary Moscow, a hellhole of graft and crime. Tania lives with her sisters, her brother, and her father in a small apartment. Her mother has recently escaped their miserable life by dying. Here, Tania addresses her mother who, we hope, is in a better place. Tania is holding a helium-filled baloon. Note: Russian accent unnecessary.

TANIA: Mom! *(Looks up.)* Mom! I can't believe that you've only been up there two weeks and you already did it. The hell's over. And I know it's because of you. What? The one that started when Father read in the paper how much Baryshnikov makes and forced me to take dance lessons after school. Mom, you know that I have two left feet, and I hate it. I mean, I wouldn't mind having talent for classical dance. But there's no way in hell. And Father's stubborn, and you know how he gets when he's stubborn. But with God's help, he started drinking again, and he didn't pay and they threw me out. Father's hiding it from me because first, he's embarrassed, and second, he's afraid I'll kill myself. Hahaha . . . *(She does a happy pirouette.)* And I cried from joy. So I bolted to the Hotel Rosija to celebrate. But when the waiter noticed I only ordered tea, he publicly made fun of me and physically threw me out. So here's my request. That I go back there. But you know, Mom, high heels, fur coat. And then I'll cuss him out. I wrote down all the details. *(She kisses the balloon and lets it go. The balloon goes up in the air. Then, Tania suddenly remembers something and jumps up to catch it. But the balloon is too high already. Annoyed:)* Aaa, well, shit. Aaa. Again I forgot about the visas because I was supposed to ask about the visas because they refuse to give them to us. And Uncle Vanya invited us to Brooklyn. So why don't you take care of that since it's easier for you. But I'll put that in the next balloon, details and all. Actually, I think it's better this way. In the last balloon, I stuffed it with so many requests, it went down instead of up.

Galaxy Video
Marc Morales

Comic

Angry Employee (twenties to thirties)

The speaker is asking the manager of a video store for her job back.

ANGRY EMPLOYEE: I met you for a short time five days ago when I came into work. It was my first day. I was in the Folk Song Musical section fixing tapes when I noticed four tapes that were in the wrong place. *Fort Apache, the Bronx, Empire Records, War Games,* and *The Way We Were. Are any of those films folk song musicals?* I don't think so. Then this woman comes over to me and asks if we had that movie that had that guy in it who was in that movie with the girl who was in that movie with that guy. *(Pause.)* At that moment I decided that I hated people. So I turned myself inward to search for an answer for what to do. I can do stuff like that: I take yoga. Quit. That was the answer. Quit. So I quit. To myself, and I walked out. I went to my therapist Doctor Kubrick, and I asked him why? Why do I hate people? He replied, "Because you hate yourself." Wow. I do hate myself. But why? Why do I hate myself? I turned myself inward once again to find the answer. *(Pause.)* My art, I have been neglecting my art. I am an artist. I draw little stick people. I draw them well. But I've been neglecting them lately because of my yoga, and work. I love drawing my little stick people. You should always make time for those things that you love to do. *(Pause.)* I am better now. May I have my job back?

I'll look good in tomorrow's photogravure.
(Young Woman assumes different poses.)

How do you want me?
It's a rhetorical question.
Fetching? Perhaps
Whimsical, capricious, coquettish to be sure
Here's Pert, Saucy, Bewitching . . . Alluring

I give you, Tantalizing, Teasing, Tempting, always.
I am by instinct.
Toss of head, angle of chin, curve of neck
Always right
Up to the orgasmic dissolve

We work well together
Where do you stop and I begin?
I await your separation
In safe-light suspension
O.K., I'm ready
Click the shutter

(Young woman becomes flustered, unsure.)

I'm all aflutter
You'd think I'd be used to this
Each time is like the first virgin thrust
One more minute,
My makeup's running, nose shiny . . .
No! I'm beauty's perfection
The stuff dreams are made of

"No sweat" as they say,
Click the shutter while the feeling rises
Take the wave at its crest

Now! Fire when ready, Sir
I'm at my best

Etta Jenks
Marlane Gomard Meyer

Dramatic

Etta (early thirties)

> Etta has come to Hollywood in hopes of becoming a star, but she
> has found that it is not as easy as she had thought. Here, she is talk-
> ing to her boyfriend, Burt.

ETTA: I think my throat is closing up. Those French fries were so dry. I
think they're caught . . . like a lump in my throat. I think those fries
got caught in my throat. I wish I had a Coke. I saw this science experiment once, where they put this tooth in Coke, and over a period of a few weeks or days . . . or maybe it was just one day, it
completely fell apart. Just disappeared. I guess that could happen with
a whole set of teeth if we were to sit around with a mouthful of Coca-
Cola day and night. I wonder how it would work, the teeth comin'
out, would you swallow and then what, would they come back in . . .
somehow? God, I'm stupid. What am I supposed to do? I thought by
now I'd at least have some kinda extra work, somethin' . . . I met this
girl, Sheir, at the lunch counter? I thought she was pretty weird but
she came out to be nice and she said that one way to break into
movies is to have a videotape of yourself made. Performing a scene
with someone or maybe doin' a monologue. But the problem is, it
costs. I wonder how I could get five hundred dollars? I had four hundred, but that's just about gone. I wonder if I could find somebody
with one of those video cameras you use at home? *(She nudges Burt, he
looks at her.)* Do you know anybody with a . . . home movie camera?

Fairy Tale Romance

M. Kilburg Reedy

Seriocomic

Woman (thirties)

> The speaker is in the midst of reading a bedtime story to her six-year-old daughter.

WOMAN: Oh, don't say that Heather. He's not a jerk. Well, your mommy is right, it's not very grown-up to pout, but he only does that because he's afraid of getting hurt. He doesn't mean to be a Beast. It's a curse his wicked stepmother put on him, and now he doesn't trust women. But if Beauty loves him enough, he'll learn to trust her, and then he won't be a Beast anymore, because he'll know that she'll never leave him.

The Beast gave Beauty a ring, and told her, "Put this on your finger when you go to sleep tonight, and it will take you home. If you decide to return, pull it off your finger, and you will be instantly returned to my palace."

When Beauty awoke the next morning, she was in her old room at home. She was overjoyed to see her father and sisters again. Soon the week was up, but Beauty did not return to the Beast's palace. Every day she said to herself, "Tomorrow I will go back," and every evening she said, "Just one more day."

Then one night she had a dream that the Beast lay dying in the garden that she knew so well. She was very upset and immediately pulled the ring off her finger before she went back to sleep. In the morning, she woke up in the Beast's palace.

Beauty was so frightened by her dream that she went to look for the Beast. She searched the palace and the grounds until at last she found him, lying in the garden. He was scarcely breathing.

"Ah, Beauty," said the Beast, "You see what has happened because you abandoned me. You are just in time to watch me die."

"Oh, please don't die, Beast," Beauty said. "I promise never to leave you again. I'll do anything to save you."

"Will you marry me, Beauty?" asked the Beast.

What do you think, Heather? Should she say yes? Beauty is the only one who can break the spell. She's the only one who can see past his horrible, Beastly exterior to the hurt little boy inside. She's the only one who can heal his wounds and make him happy.

You really think she should? But what if he doesn't turn into a Prince? What if she marries him and he's still the same old Beast, day after day for the rest of their lives?

What do you think happens in the story? That's right.

Beauty kisses the Frog, and he turns into a Prince. Wait a minute, that's not the same story. On second thought, yes it is. Beauty swallows her misgivings and kisses the Frog/Beast, and the next thing you know he's bringing her flowers, and telling her he loves her in eight different languages, and calling her when he says he's going to call, and asking her how her day went.

The next thing you know, he's actually listening to her for a change, and he really seems to care what's on her mind. Pretty soon she's relaxed, and having a wonderful time. He laughs at her jokes. She doesn't have the horrible anxious feeling that if she pauses for a moment to collect her thoughts, he'll jump in and change the subject.

Finally she starts to feel a little guilty because she's talking so much, and she says to him, "So how are *you*? Tell me how *you* are." And *he* says . . . *(She laughs, unbelievingly.)* . . . *he* says, "Oh, that's not important right now. Go on with your story." *(Sadly; to Heather.)* Now how's that for a fairy tale?

The Fourth Sister
Janusz Glowacki

Comic

Tania (twenties)

This dark comedy takes place in contemporary Moscow, a hellhole of graft and crime. Tania lives with her sisters, her brother, and her father in a small apartment. Her mother has recently escaped their miserable life by dying. Here, Tania addresses her mother who, we hope, is in a better place. Tania is holding a helium-filled baloon. Note: Russian accent unnecessary.

TANIA: Mom! *(Looks up.)* Mom! I can't believe that you've only been up there two weeks and you already did it. The hell's over. And I know it's because of you. What? The one that started when Father read in the paper how much Baryshnikov makes and forced me to take dance lessons after school. Mom, you know that I have two left feet, and I hate it. I mean, I wouldn't mind having talent for classical dance. But there's no way in hell. And Father's stubborn, and you know how he gets when he's stubborn. But with God's help, he started drinking again, and he didn't pay and they threw me out. Father's hiding it from me because first, he's embarrassed, and second, he's afraid I'll kill myself. Hahaha . . . *(She does a happy pirouette.)* And I cried from joy. So I bolted to the Hotel Rosija to celebrate. But when the waiter noticed I only ordered tea, he publicly made fun of me and physically threw me out. So here's my request. That I go back there. But you know, Mom, high heels, fur coat. And then I'll cuss him out. I wrote down all the details. *(She kisses the balloon and lets it go. The balloon goes up in the air. Then, Tania suddenly remembers something and jumps up to catch it. But the balloon is too high already. Annoyed:)* Aaa, well, shit. Aaa. Again I forgot about the visas because I was supposed to ask about the visas because they refuse to give them to us. And Uncle Vanya invited us to Brooklyn. So why don't you take care of that since it's easier for you. But I'll put that in the next balloon, details and all. Actually, I think it's better this way. In the last balloon, I stuffed it with so many requests, it went down instead of up.

Galaxy Video
Marc Morales

Comic

Angry Employee (twenties to thirties)

The speaker is asking the manager of a video store for her job back.

ANGRY EMPLOYEE: I met you for a short time five days ago when I came into work. It was my first day. I was in the Folk Song Musical section fixing tapes when I noticed four tapes that were in the wrong place. *Fort Apache, the Bronx, Empire Records, War Games,* and *The Way We Were. Are any of those films folk song musicals?* I don't think so. Then this woman comes over to me and asks if we had that movie that had that guy in it who was in that movie with the girl who was in that movie with that guy. *(Pause.)* At that moment I decided that I hated people. So I turned myself inward to search for an answer for what to do. I can do stuff like that: I take yoga. Quit. That was the answer. Quit. So I quit. To myself, and I walked out. I went to my therapist Doctor Kubrick, and I asked him why? Why do I hate people? He replied, "Because you hate yourself." Wow. I do hate myself. But why? Why do I hate myself? I turned myself inward once again to find the answer. *(Pause.)* My art, I have been neglecting my art. I am an artist. I draw little stick people. I draw them well. But I've been neglecting them lately because of my yoga, and work. I love drawing my little stick people. You should always make time for those things that you love to do. *(Pause.)* I am better now. May I have my job back?

Ghost Dance
Mark Stein and Frank Condon

Dramatic

Mrs. Blaine — a young woman, intelligent, energetic, and, as women were
in 1891, completely buttoned.

> The jail in Sioux Falls, South Dakota. Mrs. Blaine has come from
> the East, along with many others, to attend the trial of Plenty Horses,
> charged with the unprovoked killing, at point-blank range, of an
> Army lieutenant. Secretly, however, Mrs. Blaine, the daughter-in-law
> of Secretary of State James Blaine, is using the trial as a cover to hide
> from the press the fact that she is really there to get a divorce. (Based
> on actual events.)

MRS. BLAINE: My name is Mrs. Blaine. *(Awaits some acknowledgment; none
comes.)* I know a lot of women have come by to . . . view you. I'm
not one of them. I think it's very rude, in fact, to say the least. *(Then:)*
God, I sound like my mother-in-law. No wonder you're not re-
sponding. I'm here because your attorney was hoping you might talk
to me. Or, more to the point, that I might convince you to talk to
him. (Her jest gets nothing.) The reason being . . . my father-in-law
is James Blaine. *(Awaits a response; none comes.)* James Blaine, the Secretary of State? I don't know if Indians read newspapers. *(Awaits a
response; none comes.)* I only mention my father-in-law because your
case, Mr. Plenty Horses, has aroused considerable interest. *(Awaits
a response; none comes.)* Maybe not from you, but from others. *(Still
nothing.)* If you want me to leave, just say so. *(Nothing.)* Or don't.
(Nothing.) How about this? If you say nothing, I'll take that as a sign
that you want me to go. And I will. *(Nothing.)* OK. *(Starts to leave,
but then:)* Oh all right, maybe I *am* like all the others, but good God,
man, the Secretary of State! Does that mean *nothing* to you?! *(Nothing.)* Why did you shoot the lieutenant? *(Nothing.)* Do you even
know? *(Nothing.)* I suppose even if you did, why would you tell me

45

when you won't even talk to your attorney. But if it was connected, in some way, with what took place at Wounded Knee, my father-in-law, perhaps, can help. Behind the scenes, of course. A word here, a favor there. I don't know if that makes any sense to you or not. Politics? I find it fascinating but I know it's not everyone's cup of tea. *(Nothing.)* My mother-in-law, though never to my face, says I'm an opportunist. That's why I married her boy, y'see. And maybe she's right, in a way, I don't know, who *isn't* an opportunist?! *(Stops, realizing she is becoming unhinged.)* I'll be frank with you, sir. I don't know why it should make any difference to me whether or not you hang. For all I know, you deserve to. But I can't help but tell you *I think you have a chance! (Confidentially now.)* When I arrived at my hotel, and saw all the spectators gathering for your trial . . . Do you even know about that? Women especially. Which, no one wants to admit it, but when women show an interest . . . *(Realizing she's starting to get unglued again.)* Well, that's another matter. *(Takes a moment to collect herself.)* Why did you shoot the lieutenant? *(A moment then:)* I don't know why. I need to know.

Highway Ulysses
Rinde Eckert

Dramatic

Waitress (thirties to forties)

> Our hero, Ulysses, is on a journey through America. Here, he gets
> an earful from a truck-stop waitress.

WAITRESS: You aren't going to kill yourself, are you? You see, there's an
eclipse in about a half an hour. You know the moon comes between
the Earth and the Sun. Anyway. Last time there was an eclipse this
guy blew himself away and we all had to stay after for the police,
and today I got to get the kids ready or they'll miss the bus. I finally
saved enough to send them to camp, you see, and I'm off in two
hours. I can't stay late. He just needed somebody to pay attention,
you know . . . but I suppose the eclipse didn't help him very much. Are
you a scientist? I mean does it give off harmful rays that could do that?
You know some strange Sun/Moon stuff. D'you know science? . . . He
must have felt isolated, that guy. Me? I could use a little isolation,
what with the kids, and the family, that idiot brother going broke
modifying his cars, my mother with her coupon fixation, the back-
yard chicken business of Dad's — all those complaints from the
neighbors. God they get diseases. And my unlucky sister with her
enormous, unemployable boyfriend. You a vet? He was a vet. That
guy who killed himself? In just two hours when I get off I put the
kids on a bus and head up somewhere for two weeks alone, no kids.
Maybe on a mountain sitting by a stream or in it, splashing naked
in a stream in the mountains, just below the tree line — some mountain stream pooling under rocks, protected by leafage. I'll take off
my clothes and sink into the cold till I'm numb — till I can't feel
my body.

In the Wreckage
Matthew Wilson

Dramatic

Amy (twenties to thirties)

Amy alone in a sparsely furnished contemporary apartment.

AMY: Little Bastard. I'd say it to his face. I would so. If he was here, I'd say, "You're a real bastard, you bastard. You're a real son of a bitch." That's what I'd say. If he was here. Probably he'd start laughing. He'd laugh and say, "Oh, come on, I'm not so bad," and I'd say, "Yes, you are, you *are* so bad, you little bastard, you little son of a bitch," and then he'd stop laughing. He'd stop because he would know that I was serious this time. He'd know that because I'd say it to his face. If he was here.

I know what would happen next. He'd be silent a long time. He'd just stare at me while he tried to figure it all out. Then he'd look at me and say, "Now *listen* . . . " but I wouldn't be listening. Not to him. Not this time. Maybe in the past, but not anymore. I wouldn't have to listen to him anymore. He'd say, "Listen, I won't sit here and have you call me these ridiculous names." I know he would say that. That's the sort of thing he *always* said. Then I'd tell him, "You *will*, you will *absolutely* listen to me. You'll *listen* this time." Oh, it would be so sweet. So sweet to finally say that to him. I'd do it, too. Don't tell me I wouldn't. I'd say it right to his face.

That's when things would really heat up. He'd start screaming now. I'm sure of it. He'd start with the screaming, the accusations . . . He'd tell me it was all in my head. My imagination. Some nerve. Like he lived inside my head. He doesn't live inside my head. Because that was his way, you know. It was always me. It was never him. It was never his problem. The room was never too cold for him. It had to be too cold for you and could someone please turn up the heat because this other person is freezing to death. Like he could know if I was cold. He doesn't live inside my body and he shouldn't say those things. I wouldn't let him. I'd say, "It's *not* in my head, you bastard. You little son of a bitch. It was *never* in my head, it was always *you*. Stop saying in it was in my head. You don't live inside my head, do you? You don't know *what* goes on there." I'd say that to him. Damn right. He wouldn't know what to do, what to say. He wouldn't know what hit him. I can see it now. Inside my head. Because it *was* him, it *really* was, it was . . .

Oh, I don't know. I guess I don't know.

No, I *do* know and I'm *right,* and, and, and . . . IT WAS HIM. Little Bastard. That's *exactly* what I would say. If he was here.

Then he would lose it. He'd really lose it. He'd start tearing through the apartment, knocking things over. He'd keep on screaming, but I wouldn't back down. I'd tell him to take a hike. I'd tell him he was a leech, that he sucked the life right out of people, I'd tell him the whole world didn't revolve around him and his problems and I'd say it to his face. I'd look him right in the eye and tell him to quit sucking the rest of the world down in his little sinkhole. He'd yell and scream and throw things around the room and I'd stand my ground. I wouldn't give in no matter what and he'd go nuts and he'd put his fist through the window again and it would really be something.

Wouldn't it? Wouldn't that be something? That would really be something.

If he was here.

Laestrygonians
Don Nigro

Seriocomic

Jessie (eleven)

Jessie Armitage, age eleven, who lives with her parents and her sisters in a big falling apart old house in east Ohio in 1913, writes to her older brother John Rose, who is at this point an actor in a touring Shakespearean company in Britain. Jessie is a very bright little girl with a sense of humor and a great capacity for love. She adores her family, and she loves telling John about them. John is her favorite person in the world, and she misses him very much. She speaks her letter to us as if we were John — we don't see her writing.

JESSIE: June 27th, 1913. Dear Johnny. It's very hot today, and there's a thunderstorm coming, which I love, although everybody thinks I'm crazy, and Mother is afraid of storms, but sometimes I sneak out and let it rain on me until I'm soaked. When Lizzy catches me she scolds me like the dickens and tells me I'll get pneumonia but I just giggle at her and pretty soon she starts giggling, too. Lizzy has a nice laugh when she does that. I'm eleven but I act more like I'm eighteen than she does. Mother says I'm very preconscious, but I think I'm as conscious as the next person. She is well and sends her love, but as usual she and Papa barely speak to each other. Honestly, they're so grumpy sometimes. What's wrong with them? And Molly keeps snipping at me but Dorothy is my best friend because I blurt out all the things she'd say if she could talk. We all miss you very much. I still remember the night you left, but I wish I had a picture of you now, as that was many years ago when I was just a tiny little innocent child of six. Now I'm almost grown up and you're playing beggars and dead bodies and crazy people. I loved your story about how the cow kept mooing in the field while poor Mr. McDuffy was trying to be King Lear. I'm reading all the plays you're in. Molly said I just pretend to understand them so I acted Juliet's whole death scene for her and I was so good she cried. Molly is such a powder, I love her a lot. She's very pretty and boys like her. Boys don't chase Lizzy much, I don't know why. Personally I think boys are stupid and should be locked up until they're old like Papa. Please come home and visit us soon and don't forget me and send me your picture. Love, Jessie.

Laestrygonians
Don Nigro

Seriocomic

Jessie (twenty-one)

Jessie Armitage, age twenty-one, who lives with her mother and sisters in a big falling apart old house in east Ohio in 1923, writes to her older brother John Rose, a leading man in silent movies. She is a smart, funny, beautiful, magical girl, convinced that she has some special destiny waiting for her, and deeply in love with her brother John, who stays away from home and drinks too much, trying desperately to avoid beginning the physical relationship with her that neither of them can help wanting. She speaks the letter to us as if we were John — we don't see her writing as she speaks.

JESSIE: Jessie, 25 July 1923. Dear Johnny. It's so hot. On Saturdays I go to town with Jimmy Casey to see your movies at the Odessa Theatre. You're like a handsome ghost in these movies. They're not very good, but you have this dark, lost quality that makes them better than they are. I feel bad for you, because I can see pain in your eyes, while the ghosts move across the screen and old Mrs. Dooley plays the piano, which is badly out of tune. I imagine you in Hollywood, engaging in orgies with starlets. I go out with lots of boys but the only one I like is Jimmy Casey, who is quiet when I want to be quiet and crazy when I'm feeling crazy, but I see the others so Jimmy won't think he's anything special to me. He came back dangerous after the war, and I like that. Mother and Lizzy want me to marry somebody, probably not Jimmy, but I don't want to. They think I'm a loose woman, and I enjoy encouraging them in this delusion, but despite the wild reputation I'm getting, I never let boys do anything. They want to, but I scare them away with my mouth. Mother is sad and lost since Papa died. Lewis is a good husband to Lizzy, but since she lost her baby she's very crabby, and looks down on me for running around. Molly's going to marry that rascal Cletis. I look at all these boys and see that I'm wasting my life with them. Nobody compares to you, Johnny. I'm still mad at you for running off and not even saying good-bye. I let Jimmy touch my breasts sometimes when we go swimming naked in the strip mine, and one night we went pretty far, but I don't want to. It's not that I'm a nice girl. I don't want to be a nice girl. It's that I'm waiting for something. I can't help feeling like I have some special destiny. Please come home and see us, I think about you all the time, especially at night. When it's very hot, I sleep naked in your room. I miss you always. I really need to see you, Johnny. Please be safe, and don't drink so much. Love, Jessie.

The Lucky Believe
David Cirone

Dramatic

Jackie (thirties)

> After a tragic accident where his car strikes and kills a young boy,
> up-and-coming business executive Michael Ambrose wanders down-
> town in a state of shock and — on a whim — catches a Greyhound
> bus, abandoning the demands of his job and his marriage and trav-
> eling aimlessly around the country. Weeks later, his wife Jackie tells
> her sister, Sandy, about her feelings as she dresses for a "friendly" din-
> ner date with her supervisor.

JACKIE: You ever have one of those dreams? You know, one of those . . .
where you wake up and you know it was a dream, but it sticks with
you? *(No answer.)* I had this *bad* one this morning! Right before I
woke up, I dreamt he called me up, and I was in the car, driving,
and he said, "I have something to tell you." And I knew — I knew
what he was gonna say, right away. He said, "I'm getting married."
And I said, "Good luck, call me in five months when it's over." And
he laughed. And then I knew — you know how in dreams you know
things, like so completely certainly? I knew he was serious. And I
said, "You're serious," and he said "Yes." And I said — I'm like trying to make a turn in the car and I'm screaming at him, "You suck!
I hate you!" And then there was just silence. And I woke up like that.
I was in a bad mood because of this dream. I was just pissy all day.
At the bank, I totally bitched out this teller that had forgotten to
check this batch of checks for endorsement, and they're no good,
but they're already in there, so we have to do all this paperwork,
and man . . . I don't know, it just stuck with me all day. Fucking
bad day. And all because of him and he's not even here. *(Buttoning
up the dress.)* Just . . . fucking . . . not . . . right. *(Turns to Sandy.)*
There. Look at what I've done to this one.

The Mayor's Limo
Mark Nassar

Seriocomic

Martel (midtwenties to late thirties)

> Martel is a street hooker with a sassy attitude. She has been brought
> into the detective's room of a police precinct and asked what she may
> know about a case the detectives are working on.

MARTEL: I'm in the club with my friend Boop. Well, her name is Aida
but we call her Boop 'cause she looks like Betty Boop, ya know the
cartoon. She's got that nose . . .

All right! All right! Shhhhh. Shut up. So, anyway, we're supposed
to be working, but we're in this club and we did enough blow to fill
the set of Rudolph the Red Nose Reindeer and we didn't have anymore. Now, Boop starts cryin' 'cause we got no money and we're supposed to be workin'. If we come back with nothin', Reggie's gonna
kick our asses. So, Boop's hysterical. I'm ready to kill the bitch. And
then this chump steps up to the bar . . . checkin' me out. The dude's
so looped he don't even know we're hookers. He breaks out his wallet to buy a drink. It's stuffed with money. Hundreds are fallin' out
and shit. *(Sings it.)* "Money . . . money . . . money . . . money . . .
MON-ney." I start small talkin' with the guy. He thinks he's gettin'
over. So, I get on it right away. I look 'em right in the eye and I say:
"Honey, let's stop bullshittin' each other. I'm hot for you and you're
hot for me. Let's get outta here . . . let's go to my place . . . "

All right. All right. So, I say: "I'm hot for you and you're hot
for me. Let's get outta here." And let me tell ya, this motherfucker
was ugly. He was fallin' all over himself to get outta there and be with
me. So, we're outta there . . . I tell Boop ta stop cryin' and meet me
at the Big Bar. We get in this guy's BMW . . . sucker's got a BMW.
I tell 'im where to go and he starts driving. I say to him: "I can't take
it anymore, you gotta let me jerk you off." He couldn't whip it out

fast enough. He was already spottin'. I start strokin' him nice and slow. I didn't want him to blow too fast. I had his dick in one hand and I had his wallet in the other. I tell 'im: "Honey, when you come, I wanna hear you moan. I wanna hear you." Well, when he was moanin', his wallet was goin'. Then I did the old pull-over-and-let-me-get-some-cigarettes routine and I was outta there. Fifteen hundred dollars in cash, credit cards, the works. Now that's movin' . . . Guy probably didn't know what hit him. I'm tellin' ya, men are weak and stupid. And thank God, 'cause that's how I make my livin'. So, there's my proof. Men are weaker and stupider than women. Has nothin' ta do with givin' birth.

New York Water
Sam Bobrick

Comic

Linda (twenties to thirties)

> Linda is talking to an ardent suitor named Albert. Here she eluci-
> dates why any relationship with him could not possibly work out.

LINDA: You see, Albert, I am an ultra, altruistic, dedicated Liberal, and
you, it seems, you are a lowlife, scum-sucking, piece-of-vomit Con-
servative. Oh, Albert, had we only been of different races or religions,
I know it would have been semi-smooth sailing for us all the way. But
there are too many issues to overcome. Fair housing, the homeless, equal
opportunity employment, taxing the piss out of the rich . . . Slowly,
our lives will become entangled with these unsolvable problems, and
whatever love and passion there was between us will go right down
the crapper.

It will never work, Albert. We are who we are. I've learned long
ago that it isn't us that molds the city. It's the city that molds us. The
necessity to be it, to breathe it. The necessity to eat at *this* year's restaurant, to see *this* years musical . . . to permit ourselves to live in ver-
min infested, high-rent dumps, fearing constantly for our lives. The
degradation of having to journey day in and day out, in the stinking, reeking, overcrowded public transportation, filled with dis-
traught, miserable, short-tempered, Gothamites, frightened to
death to make eye contact with one another, each trying to justify
this horrendous existence just for the privilege of being able to walk
into the intimidating Metropolitan Museum two or three days a year
and laud the fact that they don't have museums like this in Peoria.
It doesn't make sense anymore, Albert. That I know. But it is our
heritage and duty to pass it on.

The Nina Variations
Steven Dietz

Dramatic

Nina (early twenties)

> *The Nina Variations* is a fascinating series of riffs on the characters
> of Nina and Konstantin Treplev in Chekhov's *The Sea Gull.* Here
> Nina is telling Treplev about a terrifying dream she has had.

NINA: I dreamt you killed yourself and no one would tell me. I asked
them — I asked your mother and Masha and Dorn, everyone —
and they all said you'd gone away. That you'd returned to the city.
That you were working on a new play. Why would I dream that?
(She looks at him. He looks at her, but says nothing.) And, in fact, when
I returned to the city, I saw your name on a marquee. A new play
of yours was to open. Your photo was in front of the theater. And
next to it, the title of your play: *Nina.* And I bought a ticket, and
went in and sat down, and I watched the play. And there were *people in it.* And *things happened in it* . . . quietly, like small quakes
within a life. And there was love. Buckets of love. And I rushed back-
stage and I cried as I embraced the actors. And I asked: "Where is
the author? Where is Konstantin Gavrilovich?" And the actress who
had played the title role — the woman who had been your Nina —
took me aside into a small room. And she took my hand. Looked
in my eyes. "The fact is . . . " — she said — "Konstantin Gavrilovich
has killed himself." *(Long silence.)* Why would I dream that?

No Niggers, No Jews, No Dogs

John Henry Redwood

Dramatic

Mattie (late thirties)

Mattie, a black woman, is talking to her husband about her love for him.

MATTIE: *(Silence. Fiery.)* For better or for worse. That's what we said eighteen years ago, and I meant it. I knew that there was going to be times when things would be bad . . . when each of us would be tested by God and man . . . when our marriage would have to face forces as powerful as a tornado sweeping across a tobacco field. But, I believed that if we just held hands and stood facing that tornado together, that we might bend . . . bend all the way down until our foreheads were almost touching the ground, but as long as we kept holding on to each other hands, we would not break. And I knew there would be times when each of us would have to face that world out there alone, but that we could stand up to anything . . . anybody, because the spirit of the other was with us. And when you came in here mad and whipped by that world out there, I stood there and said, "Give me your rage. Bring it on home to me. That's what I'm here for." Because I knew that if you tried to let that rage out outside of this house, out there in that world, those white folks would kill you. Every colored woman knows she has to be strong to be able to take on the rage her man can't let loose anywhere else. And I was strong. And I took it on . . . absorbed it . . . head on . . . point blank. *(Softly.)* And then I put my arms around you and pulled your head to my bosom and told you that it was all right; that I knew you were the man that world out there was afraid to let you be; that I never asked you to be a Superman, just my man. Then I cried for you . . . cried the tears that you were too much of a man to cry. And I did it with all the love I could muster up from the very bottom of my being. Now I'm asking you to hold my hand and face this tornado with me . . . *(Mattie puts her hand out to Rawl.)* . . . to have faith in my love for you; to help me care for and accept the responsibility that the Lord has given to grow inside me.

Omnium Gatherum

Theresa Rebeck and
Alexandra Gersten-Vassilaros

Comic

Julia (thirties to forties, black)

> Julia is a guest at a sumptuous dinner party. Having excused herself
> to use the bathroom, she returns to regale the other dinner guests
> with a description of its incredibly opulent décor.

JULIA: Well, first of all, it's very, how shall I put it . . . Big. And My God!
All those endless mirrored walls and ceilings and then on the floor,
what was that? . . . Which is all back-lit, you know so everything
just sort of glows. . . . *(Charged, a little angry.)* Girl, you have to see
it! I mean, it's big! . . . There I was, all by myself, you know, and I
suddenly became aware of this kind of infinite chorus line reflection
of me in every single mirror! I mean, I was just surrounded by ME,
hundreds of "ME's" just sitting there. And, well, I started to feel sorry,
so sorry, like I wanted to apologize but I didn't know to whom.
(Suddenly.) I mean, it's really less of a bathroom and more of a shrine
to our own shit, isn't it? . . . I was down there and I thought of my
mother and the little excursions we'd take to Bloomingdales. We'd
go up to the eighth floor where there were these little mock rooms,
all decorated to the hilt, and she'd oohh and ahhh, I mean this was
way better than a trip to the museum for her, it was more like an
archeological foray into white people's lives only you didn't have to
make small talk and pretend you were cozy. See, she wished that all
that luxury could be mine one day, 'cause that was a sign of real
achievement to her. But for me, hanging out in that ballroom you
call a bathroom, well, it just made me feel so far away from her and
so far away from anything real — look, no offense, Suzie, but don't
you think having a gloriously appointed bathroom is the strangest
barometer of fulfillment you could ever imagine?

Orange Lemon Egg Canary

Rinne Groff

Seriocomic

Henrietta (twenties to thirties)

> Henrietta was a magician's assistant, and she is dressed as such. I
> use the word *was* because Henrietta is a ghost. In this monologue,
> addressed directly to the audience, she talks about magic and love.

HENRIETTA: It's easy to get stuck. I got stuck the same way it happens to
any other person: by accident. I was studying to be a nurse . . . hey,
I could have been a nurse. One day after classes, my friend, my fiancé, if you're a stickler for details, took me to see a Magic Show.
Boy oh boy, this magician. He did the usual tricks, the usual stuff —
billiard balls, cards, ummmnn, cigarettes, the classics — but it was
my first time. I had never seen, I, I, I, had never even heard of a
profession like that. I was knocked, completely. I was sitting like
this . . . *(She makes a slight open-mouthed expression.)* That's probably why he chose me, called me to the stage. The stage! Plus he liked
to call on girls in the audience who had their boyfriends in tow. Their
fiancés. Stickler. He said pick a card, any card. *(Whispering.)* The
Queen of Hearts. I held it close to my breast. *(Full-voice again.)* He
told me to sit on it. Excuse me? He provided the chair. "Wait," he
said, "Face up," and he reached his hand under my thigh. He pulled
the card, without looking at it, naturally, flipped it, and slid it back
under. Then he asked me to part my lips. Okey-dokey. "Open your
mouth wider." Yeah, sure. My fiancé's watching this. He took a small
telescope and slipped it inside my open mouth, just a bit, just enough
to give me the taste of metal. When I laughed, my teeth came down
on it. "Careful," he said. "Be careful." I looked into his eyes. He gazed
down my throat, saw straight through every part of my insides, and
he guessed my card. He knew my card all right.

Orange Lemon Egg Canary
Rinne Groff

Seriocomic

Henrietta (twenties to thirties)

> Henrietta was a magician's assistant, and she is dressed as such. I use the word *was* because Henrietta is a ghost. In this monologue, addressed directly to the audience, she talks about magic and love.

HENRIETTA: And that's what I mean by "stuck."

Wires? Is that what you're thinking? Or magnets. Or mirrors. But where would the mirrors be, sharp guy, and why didn't she crash through them when she came in? How could she perform the wire rigging so quickly and impromptu? In the middle of a restaurant? How in BeJesus's name do you think magnets could help the situation?

Give over. Give over. Trust me: You might as well give over.

I've got a mark on my back, too, more horribler than hers, believe me, but I was raised in such a way . . . call me old-fashioned, but it's not polite to strip. I may have worked the theaters, but I was never a roundheel and I won't be displaying any telling marks on my torso any time soon.

Picture it: the Hypnotic Balance. A scantily clad girl — and this was between the world wars, mind you, when deshabillé, that's what they call it in France, still meant something — perfectly balanced and serene on a sturdy, protruding, spikey shaft. Great spins me around, chanting spells in my ear. It still gives me goosebumps. Commitment, faith, trust — why not? — love. There I said it. Don't move, don't even blink or the spike just might thrust right on up through you. Don't you want to see that? Don't you want it? Love.

Out to Lunch

Joseph Langham

Seriocomic

Waitress (twenties to forties)

A waitress is talking to the busboy about her annoying customers.

Lights follow Waitress to the Busboy who doesn't respond to her.

WAITRESS: garsh, will they ever leave? how long have they been here? is it still Sunday? i'm not even sure it's Sunday anymore. i think it could be Monday or Tuesday. who knows it may be the next Sunday for all I know. they have been here for so long, it could already be three Sundays from now. it's always the same, don't they have food at their houses? don't they have coffee? i hate campers, do you know what a camper is? it's people who come in here and stay here until the friggin' judgment day. they can see that we have a line of customers outside. they know that this is the busiest day of the week. they don't care. all they think of is their friggin' selves. you know what i hate worse than campers? nothing. i really can't think of anything. i think i'd rather have red hot metal toothpicks shoved under my fingernails, then stick my hands in a bucket of lime juice, and rinse with boiling salt water, do you see? do you see how much i hate campers? i would give up this miraculous manicure if they would just leave. see? see my nails? they are perfect. *(She looks at her own nails admiringly. then shock.)* holy frig! I BROKE A GALDANG NAIL! i bet i broke it on the coffeepot. or on the dessert stand. *(She begins to sob.)* it's them. it's all their fault. they broke my nail and they don't care. and, to top it all off, do you know what the worst part of them is? they don't tip. don't they know i only get paid $2 an hour? don't they know i have rent to pay? and manicures! how can i fix this nail if they don't tip? they take up your table for a friggin' decade and then leave you doody! and now . . . and now . . . they want more coffee.

64

do you hear me? have you heard a word i said? are you deaf? can you speak english? hello? hello? *(She walks around the Busboy leeringly.)* .my, my you are a big one. i bet you are the biggest busboy in the world. nice tush honey. *(She pats his tush. He doesn't react.)* i'll meet you back in the walk-in right now, big boy. i'm not wearing any panties. you can have your way with me on the butter buckets . . . hello? ah frig you!

The Pavilion
Craig Wright

Dramatic

Kari (thirties)

> While attending her high school reunion, Kari has run into her first love from high school, Peter, with whom she shares a tender memory of happier times.

KARI: Do you remember that day in the spring of junior year . . . ? It was really hot . . . and you came and got me out of study hall and we skipped out and went to The Sandwich Hut for a crunch cone? And we walked down here by the lake, and I told you I was hot, and you *picked me up.* Do you remember that?

You picked me up *just like in a movie* and you kinda dipped me back into the water so I could get my hair wet. And when you did that . . . I saw the sunshine upside down making . . . glittering little bubbly patterns on the water, like I was on a Ferris wheel, kind of, and, boom! It was like all the feelings in the lower parts of my body swooshed back up into my head, and as you lifted me up out of the water, I tilted up and all my thoughts, swoosh, all my sensibility rushed down into my underwear and I looked at you and you looked so handsome, Peter, I just suddenly knew it was the right time. And I felt so silly because just like ten minutes before I had said all that stuff to you about how I was always going to be a virgin, and I *just* didn't see why people thought sex was *so* important. And we walked back to my house holding hands and your hand was shaking so hard. *God. (Brief pause.)* To be held like that, at that age; to see those shining things; and to walk that mile with you right down the middle of the street . . . I don't want to lose that. I don't want the universe to start over. I just want to let it *go.* I want to let it go *on.* OK? OK?

The Pavilion
Craig Wright

Dramatic

Kari (thirties)

> Kari is attending her high school reunion, where she has run into
> her high school boyfriend, Peter. Neither's life has turned out the way
> they had hoped. Here, she is telling Peter about her husband, Hans.

KARI: Listen to this and maybe you'll find a way. This morning, Hans was
inside me, right? — just listen, he was inside my *body.* If there's anybody else on Earth I can tell this to, it's you. I get one life, right, and
one body, and this morning Hans was inside it. And we were all fin-
ished, but he was still on top of me and I could tell he was thinking about something. So I said, like a dope, "What are you thinking
about?" And he said, "A really difficult hole." And it wasn't even a
joke. That's what I live with. Me and that, alone every night in a split-
level pro shop with beds for the human beings to rest on in between
rounds! On a good day, it's bearable. On a bad day, you don't know.
He's *so* mad, Peter. In his mind, he rescued me from the jaws of ill
repute, right, because you'd dumped me and I'd had an abortion and
"oh God," right, and he brought me out to be the Baroness Von Nine
Iron of the most beautiful executive golf course in Becker County!
And he *did* rescue me, kind of, see, that's the real problem, he did!
And he was really sweet about it too, I mean, I can see his point, because I had been really lonely ever since you broke up with me, and
Hans was so chivalrous about it, he took me out around town like
it was all perfectly normal even though everybody always looked at
us funny. One time he took me to The Voyager and he announced
to the whole bar that we were getting married and he bought everyone a round of drinks. And Arne Neubeck was really drunk, like he
always is, and he came over and said to Hans, "You just made the
biggest . . . fucking . . . mistake of your life." And Hans punched

him so fast and so hard, he knocked the wind out of that entire room and I got a dozen roses the next day from Arne with an apology. So Hans was really sweet, and he rescued me, and all he ever wanted from me in return, the way he sees it, all he ever wanted from me was a "motherfucking baby" . . . and I wouldn't give him one, and *I won't give him one,* and his parents are all pissed off at me about it, but he's too nice to leave me and I can't change, it's just . . . *bad!* It's such an *awful bad home.*

Playing House
Brooke Berman

Dramatic

Wendy (midforties to early fifties)

> Wendy is a very strong and practical healer. Here, she describes how she found her calling.

WENDY: This is how I became a healer. I went to Hell and I came back with a gift. I came back able to see into people and objects and the Earth and to move things inside of them. But, first I was in Hell. Like you. And, it was bad. I didn't get out of bed for a long time. I pretended I was a bear and that it was winter, and I hibernated. I went on food stamps and unemployment, and I sold things. Just to support my sleep habit. But I trusted and did what my insides told me to. I took naps all the time, every day. And I cried a lot. In bed, in the bathtub, in Central Park, in the A & P buying groceries. Actually, I never shopped at the A & P, but you know what I mean, right? Anyway, miraculous things began to occur. While I was asleep, the light got in and moved things inside of me. It was amazing. The healing occurred while I was not conscious. I woke up and had this gift. And I'd always had it only I couldn't find it before. But once I found it, I could use it to help people. To set them on their path. I believe in change. I believe in healing. I believe you can make great progress in this life.

Rocket Man
Steven Dietz

Dramatic

Louise (early forties)

> Louise is in love with Donny (with whom she works as a surveyor) whose wife, Rita, has left him for another man. She seeks solace in religion. That's the first act. The second act, in which this monologue occurs, is about how everyone's life might have been different, had Donny made different life choices.

LOUISE: It's odd. When I look back, I remember it as the night I couldn't pray.

I left Donny standing there in his attic, and I drove home.

The house was dark.

I sat in my favorite chair.

I closed my eyes.

And I tried to pray.

But my mind kept racing — as though I were trying to sleep, the same relentless pounding in my head — and, try as I might, I couldn't quiet it.

I couldn't hear the sound of my own thoughts.

I turned on the lamp, looking for something to read.

And there beside me was Donny's portfolio.

I opened it.

And — one by one — I spread his designs and drawings all over the floor.

I sat for hours staring at them.

Alone, in my house.

Surrounded by worlds.

When Rita called the next morning, I was still sitting there.

And I closed my eyes.

And I prayed.

Rocket Man

Steven Dietz

Dramatic

Rita (early forties)

When we first met Rita, in the first act, she was estranged from her husband, Donny. Here, they are back together because the second act of this fascinating play is about the "what-ifs" of life as in, what if we took a different path rather than the one we in fact took. Here, Rita is talking to her husband, Donny. Apparently, their lives' actions are heading what we in our universe would call "backwards."

RITA: I have maps, Donny. I have a LOT of maps. I've been collecting them since the day we got married. And I saved these maps so that one day — when we plan our honeymoon — we can decide where we want to go —

A honeymoon is the last act of a marriage — one final adventure before we're swallowed up by youth. It's a *culmination,* Donny. And maybe that's what we need. A "practice honeymoon." A trip to look at our lives before we get any younger.

A chance for you to start over. Now, look at these and decide. I'll go anywhere you want — but we've got to go *somewhere.* We've got to get you out of this house.

Here's the itinerary. Tell me what you think. OK. I thought we'd start with the arboretum you did — your first big job — laid out like the stars in Orion. Then we'll visit the gardens you did back East — the Corona Borealis. Then the park that won all the awards — based on Aquila — "The Eagle." And we'll end up at that project you abandoned, the design that was going to be your *crowning achievement:* the Steps to the Sea. They never hired another architect, you know. They're still waiting for you — just like I am.

Donny, you sit in the café, day after day, staring out the window, scribbling away on napkins — *it's like you're drifting away, and*

I'm trying to make sense of it. One year ago, you stopped working. And you never told me why. You said maybe, someday, you'd start again — but when? If you wait any longer, you'll be *too young* — you'll have too little time left. *(Moving to him, looking in his eyes.)* There's a *window,* Donny. A window of time for everything in our lives. And if we let that window close, that part of us is gone. I wish you'd say something because I really want a cigarette and I'm too mad to kiss you.

Sally's Gone, She Left Her Name

Russell Davis

Dramatic

Sally (teens)

Sally, a very passionate teenager, is talking to her mother.

SALLY: No, come on, Mom. I'm not waking Dad. *(Pause.)* Mom, I'm sorry. I get restless. In this house. I do. I don't know how you can stay so quiet like this. I just feel like blurting. I don't want to turn out this way. What we are in this house. This way of thinking. This is not the way we should be, you and I, in this world. All comfortable. While Dad gives shelter. No, I get restless thinking like that. Mom, I do. I want something more. I want what Grandpa had. What made him poor. I want how he painted.

Like that girl.

I want to be the girl Grandpa painted.

More than anything I know I want to be like that picture. Something like that picture.

Then I'd get to wear that wide headband she's got around her head.

And that white gown that's so light you can see the nighttime through it.

It floats. Like a veil.

I want to run out like that in the middle of the night. To the ocean, more than anything I know. Far away from any town, or teachers, family, or house. Just run up and down. Yes. Visit the mountains and hills. Wander the wilderness. Hear my voice cry. Clap my hands and sing. Because I think if I could do that, be some kind of little girl spirit all over again, do that and not miss all the stuff, everything in my life, the people, things to do, then I would be happy.

Happy in a way for sixty years or so until I die. Go off to some other world. Wearing nothing but this same white gown and a headband. Except on my head I've embroidered: "Sally's gone."

That's right. Sally's gone.

And she left her name, so don't try calling after her.

She's left her name.

Sally's Gone, She Left Her Name

Russell Davis

Dramatic

Sally (teens)

> Here Sally is talking to her brother about their mother, who has been
> acting disengaged, to say the least, since she got out of the hospital.

SALLY: I miss Mom coming into my room at night. Telling us about Dad.
How she met Dad. And what her parents thought. *(Pause.)* I miss
Mom's stories too. What she made up. About that little girl. Who
had a moat. She saw a moat all around her. Between her and the rest
of the world. Her own body even. Like she was locked up by herself, all alone in her mind. There was nothing she could do to cross
that moat. Nobody to rescue her. And when she became a woman,
no man on Earth, no prince of this world, could win her. The more
they tried, the deeper her moat.

    Until she decided to go off in the middle of the night. Sneak
away from her land. Go to the end of the Earth. When the Earth
was still flat. And rest herself, sit on the edge of the Earth, maybe
drop off. Disappear. And nobody would know, or be to blame. But
on her way she ran out of roads. And saw what looked like a sleeping beast. Between her and the edge of the Earth. And just as she
was about to sneak around, this beast woke and grabbed her. Began
to shriek. Each time the beast shrieked, a piece of the Earth broke
off until she was about to fall herself. But someone must have caught
her. Because she woke up. In an enchanted forest. And in this forest she could see there was no moat. *(Pause.)* Ragatelle. I loved to
hear about Ragatelle. Who saw a moat. Mom's stories about the sleeping beast. Ragatelle's adventures in a forest. The wizard she met. How
Ragatelle never had to go back to the land she came from. Where

she could see that moat. *(Pause.)* I think when we were all in that car and Mom got hurt, I don't think it's because Mom banged her head like that against the car door. Whereas the rest of us were fine. Just walked away. I don't think some door which closed on her put Mom in a coma. No. Because I remember coming to the hospital, thinking how can Mom's body, or what she thinks, be so flimsy? How could Mom leave us alone like this? Why is it my mom who has to see some sleeping beast? My mom who hears this shriek? How can I ever possibly understand, how can it be explained now, what I might have to someday see myself at the end of this world? *(Pause.)* Oh, I know Mom's out of the hospital now. Sees a doctor. Has therapy. But I don't think they know what's up with Mom. How to put her back. I think Dr. Heisel just likes her. He calls. Misses her when she doesn't make an 2. But he doesn't know about Mom. How she looks ahead. How she can see right past. What feels so solid to all the rest of us.

Second Lady
M. Kilburg Reedy

Seriocomic

Mrs. Erskine (forties to fifties)

> Mrs. Erskine is the wife of a vice-presidential candidate, talking to a large group of women and reporters at a political banquet.

> *She picks up the beginning of her speech again, puts on her glasses, and reads.*

MRS. ERSKINE: "The League of Women Voters can provide the leadership needed to develop the National Community. Throughout your history you have met each challenge of the cause of democracy. I offer you another challenge, perhaps the greatest one you have yet faced."

(She puts down her glasses, then cracks up laughing.) I could just about die of embarrassment saying things like that. I can hardly keep from blushing sometimes.

(Becoming quite giddy.) Do you want to know the funniest thing about it? I happen to know that this speech was originally written for the Rotarians. My husband just inserted "League of Women Voters" wherever "Rotary Club" appeared. Were you feeling flattered and pleased to know that you have consistently "met each challenge of the cause of democracy"? Sad to say, those glowing words of praise were never meant for you at all.

(She turns to the photos behind her.) I don't know how they keep a straight face. I really don't. And they all do it, you see, all those men. Republicans do it more than Democrats — they seem to be born with a nose for the historical impact of a phrase. But most Democrats pick it up, too, after they've been around for a while, and they start to talk just the same.

Even Joseph will sometimes say things to me in a tone of voice that makes me think he is half expecting me to write it all down. He gets this very intense look in his eyes, and he'll say something like: "I'm going to change the face of this country's social welfare system."

It makes me want to look around the room to see if anyone else is there. Of course no one is, but who is he talking to when he says things like that? Not only to me. I get the feeling sometimes that I'm there to be a witness. That I'm supposed to carry his private words and deeds with me until it's time to pass them on to posterity. *(On the word "posterity," she throws a paper airplane she has constructed from the first page of her speech.)*

Shoot

David Cirone

Dramatic

Rachel (eighteen)

> Rachel, the school's most notorious tough girl, arrives at her friend's house, her grocery store uniform covered in blood. She confesses that her attempts to reconcile with her alcoholic mother have finally come to an end.

RACHEL: I tried moving back in and giving her space and saying "yes" all the time, and she's still beating on me! You know? Always gotta have her hands on me, like my shoulders, my hair . . . And today — today after work, she came up to me, she didn't even let me in the fucking door, and her breath . . . there was like a ton of beer on her breath, and I knew what it was gonna be like so I said fuck it, let me just go over Nik's, you know? I'll shower later, whatever. She's talking to me, and I'm like "whatever," and I turn around and she punched me — the bitch punched me, right in the back! And I'm like, I'm thinking I'm not twelve anymore, why is she fucking around? Doesn't she know? She's only like up here on me, and I'm . . . I still can't believe she punched me, and I sorta fell down the steps and she threw her drink at me, and now I'm covered in her stinking alcohol, and I just wanna get in there and change cuz there's no way I'm coming over here or going anywhere smelling like her, and when I go past her, she grabs me right here, where she fucking bruised me. And she threw me onto the couch and — you know I hate that fucking couch and how it smells and when I hit it, the arm — like where you put your arm — came off again. And when she pushed me again, I smacked her with it. And she kept grabbing me, so I swung at again, I had to keep hitting her until . . . *(Pause.)* . . . until she backed off. So she just cursed at me and went into the room and passed out. *(Pause.)* And I'm thinking — it's over. After all those years of trying to stay out of it, that it wasn't . . . It wasn't gonna ever work out. *(Pause.)* So I just got the fuck outta there.

Smashing
Brooke Berman

Comic

Clea (early twenties)

> Clea has traveled to London with her friend Abby to provide moral
> support for Abby, who plans some sort of revenge against a novelist
> who made his sexual liaison with her when she was a teenager into
> a best-selling novel. Clea also has a Madonna fixation, to put it mildly.
> Here, she is going on about Madonna to Nicky, a night clerk in a
> fleabag hotel where she and Abby are staying.

Clea sits at the lobby desk where Nicky works. She can't sleep.

CLEA: She makes it OK for a girl to be ambitious. To want. She takes things
we think of as "bad" — ambition, sex, Catholicism — and reinvents
them . . .

NO TALENT? How can you say no talent!? I'm going to pretend you didn't say that. What about postmodernism and appro-
priations? Gender iconography in the late twentieth century? She
didn't just do yoga. She did Kabbalah. She did burning crosses. She
vogued.

And she did Evita. The Argentines freaked, but controversy feeds
her whole deal.

The tabloids say, Madonna: Has She Gone Too Far? But I say,
Is there such a thing? Is there such a thing when you are Madonna
and the world is your oyster because you never let anyone tell you
who to be or what to do or what your limitations are? No. No. There
is no such thing. Get into the groove. Open your heart. Express yourself, don't repress yourself. Music makes the people come together.
The Bourgeoisie and the Rebel.

Yes. We have a lot in common. Her and me, not you and me
though maybe you and me have a lot in common too, I don't know

yet, but her and me, she and I, we have a bond. We're both from Detroit. And that's not all. The list goes on and on.

Loads of very creative people come from Detroit. Like Madonna and Diana Ross and me. And cars are made there. So you see. We are deeply connected by our Root Geography. And, OK this sounds fantastic but it's true — we were tigers in another life and she scratched my eyes out. It's OK though.

Smashing

Brooke Berman

Comic

Clea (early twenties)

> Clea has traveled to London with her friend Abby to provide moral support for Abby, who plans some sort of revenge against a novelist who made his sexual liaison with her when she was a teenager into a best-selling novel. Clea also has a Madonna fixation, to put it mildly. Here, she is going on about Madonna to Nicky, a night clerk in a fleabag hotel where she and Abby are staying.

CLEA: Well, waiting for Madonna to give birth. But also, see, I'm actually her illegitimate secret daughter from the early days in Detroit and I need to let her know that I exist, which I plan to do when I find her in downward facing dog at the yoga center. Or at her house, when I slip a note with my half of the secret locket, the one my adopted mom gave me when I turned eighteen, to her doorman.

No, I'm totally lying. Really, really what happened is: *(In one big gulp.)* Jason Stark, he's this writer Abby lost her virginity with when she was sixteen, he wrote a book about her and called her in the middle of the night to let her know that the book has come out and it's like, essentially all about how much she sucked as a person, but how he wants her anyway, and he needs her to be with him because he's losing his mind or something, and I'm here because I am her best friend. But Abby was retarded and didn't tell Jason we were coming so we got here and he was, I don't even know where he is, but I don't have any money, I mean, I have like ten pounds or something for the whole weekend, after paying for this place. So, he has to show up soon so I can eat. Abby doesn't eat, but I like need to.

String Fever
Jacquelyn Reingold

Dramatic

Lily (late thirties to forties)

> Lily (played by Cynthia Nixon in the original New York production) is here talking to her estranged husband Matthew, who left her to find himself, and who she hasn't seen in a long time.

LILY: *(Out/in her head.)* I have tried to move on it's not like I haven't tried I have. It's a mystery. I mean, it's bottomless. Makes no sense. I want to touch you so bad my hands are shaking, and I can't eat, I'm starving and, well, out of my mind, really, which makes me think there's not that much difference, you know, between us, I keep mine hidden, well so do you, but not a day goes by Matt that I don't crave you that I don't have to have you that I wouldn't stick you up my nose or in my arm, if I could only crush you into a powder, melt you in a spoon or drink you from a cup. You are in brightly lit close-up and there's nothing else and no matter how you've changed or how you really look I see the answer, I see this house, I see what I saw when we first met, even if you're frowning I see that smile those eyes that promise that said being close to you would make it better. I keep thinking you're still him, not someone else, not one of those people you feel sorry for. And I can't put the two together. *(To him.)* So, I want to know why I'm here. I want to know what's going on. Let's talk.

String Fever
Jacquelyn Reingold

Dramatic

Lily (late thirties to forties)

> Lily is having drinks with her father. She is telling him about a man
> she is dating, a physicist whose specialty is "String Theory." In learn-
> ing about this arcane theory in physics she has been helped to make
> some sense of her life.

LILY: I think it's strings, too. I think it is. I think I love that it's strings.
That it's a symphony, that it's incomprehensible, that it makes sense
and it makes no sense, that every time you think you have an answer you end up with another question, that we're made up of fila-
ments that vibrate in hidden dimensions that no matter how hard
you look you can't see, that it matters, that the tiniest vibrations matter, and that that people think about these things, that Frank does,
and that even though I can't for the life of me understand even a frac-
tion of it, I can understand something that I didn't use to. That meet-
ing Frank has changed the way I see things. And that I want you to
get along. Cause I love you, Dad, and I want it to work. And I really like him. I liked him instantly. OK? And I want you to see that.
Cause it matters. What's happening here, matters.

Till We Meet Again
Colin and Mary Crowther

Comic

Wife (any age)

A young woman has asked an older woman what it's like being married.

WIFE: It's like sharing your bed with a red hot limpet who commandeers three-quarters of the mattress — and the duvet — while you cling desperately to the very edge. You freeze and he sweats. Halfway through the night, when you've just sunk into unconsciousness beneath six inches of permafrost, he wakes up, flings the bedding on the floor, complains he's far too hot and insists that you — you, please note — should get up and open a window to let the rest of the Siberian gale — on to *your* side of the room. Then he screws himself into a tiny ball with his bottom stuck right over your side. And starts to snore. Not a gentle snore — with a regular rhythm you can half-pretend is a lullaby, oh no. You suddenly find you're in a pigsty with one little piggy going snortle, snortle, another little piggy going snuff, snuff. Total, blissful silence from the third piggy-wiggy. Till the fourth little porker breaks out with a trumpet blast. At that point, you realize, your feet are like slabs of ice. His are like red hot irons. You think, I'll have a bit of that heat. So you stretch out, very gently, ever so carefully, place your cold feet on his hot feet and he jumps and kicks and then it's like having a mule in the bed. And thus, more stunned than asleep, you finally close your stinging eyes, in a coma of exhaustion . . . when the alarm goes off. It's time to get up. Only you can't, 'cos you're frozen stiff and your joints have locked and your head's splitting open. So, take your choice, love. Sleeping with a man's like sleeping with a limpet, a pig, or a mule. And sometimes, all three.

Tristan
Don Nigro

Dramatic

Bel (forty)

> Bel Rhys Rose, age forty, a fragile woman who has at various times in her life been moderately insane, appears in a white nightgown, a small light before her, as if illuminated by candlelight, in the Gothic old Pendragon house in east Ohio, in the year 1887. Bel is actually telling us about her own death. Bel is the daughter of a mad carnival operator turned preacher, was assaulted on a tent organ as a girl, married by her dead brother's best friend mostly out of pity, gave birth to dead triplet. She has managed to raise her son and counterfeit something like sanity for a number of years until a mysterious lost girl, Alison, shows up on the doorstep in a rainstorm. This girl reminds her of an old love of her husband's, and Alison's presence in the house preys upon Bel's mind and leads her to have the homicidal thoughts that will lead to her own death.

Bel, in a white nightgown, in the midst of darkness, a small light before her, illuminating her face as if from a candle.

BEL: Night in the dark old house. All in the dark the dragon's foul tongue speaks to me, whispers to go to her room. I slip out of bed, careful not to wake my foolish husband, and creep up the steps with my candle before me, all ahead and behind is darkness. The door to her room is not locked. I open it carefully and go in. Sound of the ticking clock by her bed. An owl in the tree by her window. At the foot of her bed I shine the candle down upon her. Oh, she is so lovely, sleeping there, I can hardly breathe. She looks so innocent. I want to hold her in my arms and comfort her, but the dragon whispers in my ear that she is the sorceress come back to kill us. Burn the witch, whispers the dragon. Burn the witch now. His breath is fire in my head. I hesitate, I resist. Innocent child. Dreaming of her lover, she cannot see his face. But I must be strong. Then another voice comes from the doorway, and it startles me, as anything that's not inside my head can startle me, and I turn briefly and there is Sarah, in her nightgown, Sarah, who hears everything in the house, whose job has always been to keep me out of trouble, my faithful protectress since she was a little girl, who heard me creeping up the steps or saw the light from the candle flash under her door as I passed by, and as I turn, the candle drops from my hand, not on the bed of the sleeping girl, but onto my own nightgown, and in a moment everything is on fire, I am burning, breath of the dragon, burning from below, and somebody is screaming, it must be me, and then Sarah is screaming and then Alison is screaming and Sarah's trying to get me to roll on the floor, but the dragon whispers that the pond is cool and dark, so I smash through the ancient windowpane and roll down the steep roof, burning, and fall to the roof below it, burning, and then off again onto the grass, and then I am running and falling, stumbling and crawling toward the water, and the dragon's breath is roaring in my ears, and then there is the water and the ecstasy of darkness closing over me and the dragon has taken me into his mouth has entered into me and has devoured me deep under the water, and the burning is gone, and there watching me in the water I see the eyes of the lost beloved dead I have come to join, and everything is lost, and somehow it is all quite perfect.

Tristan
Don Nigro

Dramatic

Bel (forty)

> Bel Rhys Rose, a recently dead woman of forty, wanders the Gothic
> old east Ohio Pendragon mansion that was her home, a ghost now,
> observing with great interest the passions and disasters of the living
> people all around her, and attempting to understand the relation-
> ship between the living and the dead. Her son Rhys has just had a
> terrible quarrel with her husband Gavin, who fell and hit his head.
> As the others fuss and worry, Bel, now released to some extent from
> such passions, watches them and tries to understand.

BEL: Having had such a wonderful opportunity to observe the living so
closely after my untimely but spectacular demise, I'm finding myself more and more both fascinated and appalled by their almost com-
plete inability to focus on what actually matters in any given situation.
Once you're dead, this is no longer a problem. You can focus re-
markably well from inside a coffin — I mean on the basic themes
and images, the central line of action in the complex and multileveled
theater, upon what's left when the body decomposes and all else, quite
literally, falls away. Now, look at this, for example. The woman comes
between, the son nearly kills the father. I know this story. I'm sure
it must have been in one of my crazy father's books, before we fed
it to the goat, or maybe we saw it that time we went up to Cleve-
land to hear that woman with the huge ass shrieking opera. We live
out these patterns. Our lives are an infinitely complex series of in-
terlocking plays, stretching back and forth through time and infin-
ity, the major characters of one play being the spear-carriers in
another. We play in comedy one night, tragedy the next, sometimes
both at the same time. I've allowed one of these men to ejaculate
into my body, and been kicked in the stomach from the inside by

the other one, and then pushed him out into the world amid the damnedest screaming bloody mess you ever saw, but I pity most the women, who carry the massive burden of life inside them, all to be lost, all lost. It's rather beautiful, when viewed from a certain aesthetic distance, but when you get up close you can't see anything. Life is too close while we're living it to make any sense out of. Death gives us a much better perspective, but by then it's too late to do a damned thing about anything. And that's the beauty of it. All lost things are beautiful, and all beautiful things are lost. What a shame. And yet, how interesting.

Waiting
Lisa Soland

Seriocomic

Cindy (twenty-one)

Cindy is a twenty-one-year-old college student who is sexually active. Youthful in age and in her level of wisdom. Talks with a perky, rhythmic stream of consciousness. At rise, an older woman Linda, is waiting to use the bathroom.

CINDY: *(Enters and crosses to Linda.)* You waiting? [*(Linda nods.)*] Oh. OK. *(Cindy steps into line close behind Linda and appears uncomfortable. A long silence as Cindy and Linda wait.)* I'm usually not this impatient. It's just that I'm getting a urinary track infection and when I get those it hurts to wait. I mean, really hurts. I'm very sorry. *(Continuing.)* I also don't think very clearly when I'm in this kind of pain. I mean, it's an icky kind of pain. *(Beat.)* I shouldn't have waited this long to try to find a bathroom. I shouldn't have waited this long to see a doctor. *(Quickly and loudly.)* God, what is taking this woman so freakin' long? What's up with that? Why can't women just pee and get the hell on with their lives. *(We hear the toilet flush from inside the woman's bathroom. Quickly covering her own mouth with her hand.)* Oh God, she probably heard me. *(Beat.)* That's another symptom of an approaching urinary track infection — I have no control over my mouth either. *(Loudly, as if to woman in bathroom.)* Just have to pee, that's all. Just have to pee. *(Beat.)* The last time I got one of these, I was nearly hospitalized 'cause I waited too long to go to the doctor. I was trying to heal it "homeopathically." With cranberry juice. That's what they tell you to do. I drank so much freakin' cranberry juice that I developed sores on the inside of my upper lip from the acid. Who would have known. Too much of a good thing. Never again. 'Course I say never again and here I am. *(Beat.)* It was on Valentine's Day. My friend, Eric finally took me to campus emergency 'cause I couldn't physically drive, or stand up straight, for that matter. My boyfriend at the time, was out with his mother, so he said. *(Beat.)* They I-V'd me and everything. My white blood count was sky high and they told me I had a kidney infection and it was bad. *(Thinking back.)* They scolded me. Do you believe it?! A twenty-one-year-old woman and they're talking to me as if I'm some kind of kid. *(Beat.)* They asked me if I was a dance major and I said "no." I guess dancers get them because of the tights they gotta wear. I said, "No, just starting another relationship." *(To self.)* Just starting another relationship. *(Beat.)* I get them when I start sleeping with a new partner. I guess my body isn't used to it or something and I get them, but he finally showed up. *(Beat.)* My boyfriend. *(Explaining.)* The one at the time. *(Continuing, with a pleasant memory.)* And he had this big ol' heart-shaped box of Lady Godiva chocolates and I was starved, so we sat there and ate them together while the nurse came in and out poking me. And he kept telling me all these stupid jokes I had already heard a million times. *(Beat.)* From him. *(Beat.)* I mean, what's up with that?! *(Beat.)* It's like they don't even remember they told you them and it makes me feel like I could be anybody. Just anybody lying there in the emergency room. *(Beat.)* I tried to laugh but I kept thinking, "This isn't funny. Why does he keep trying to make me laugh?" *(They wait, then to Linda.)* Very painful. I get them all the time. It sucks really. I don't know what's up with that. *(Beat.)* They tell you if you pee just before you have sex, or just after sex, that that will take care of the problem. I guess it's some sort of "healthy preparation," but it doesn't work. It doesn't work. I've tried it. I've tried everything. *(Blackout.)*

Waiting
Lisa Soland

Dramatic

Linda (thirties)

> Linda, thirty to forty years old, is married to Steve, a paraplegic in a wheelchair. Due to her husband's handicap, she has seen a darker, unaccepting side of humanity. She is mainly talking to Truman, an eighty-three-year-old man who has innocently asked about their life together.

LINDA: *(Out of the silence, she begins to speak.)* You know, the pain never comes from where you expect it to come from. If it did, then it would be easy. Life would be easy. But it doesn't. It comes from where you don't expect it. It sneaks up behind you when you're not looking and it takes your heart and stretches it in directions you . . . really wouldn't want it to go. *(Beat.)* You see, you'd expect me to be sad about him, that he can't walk or do anything for that matter, because this is . . . a life of action. It's an active world. *(Sarcastically.)* Hell, everything worth while requires action. Right? So you'd think I'd be in pain about that. There's hiking, camping skiing, traveling, sight-seeing . . . But I'm not. That doesn't bother me. *(To Steve.)* It doesn't bother me, honey. It never has. *(Continuing.)* And if I was like most pigs I've seen, like that . . . *(Almost insinuating Cindy's breasts.)* . . . "perky" co-ed we . . . experienced earlier, I would be upset because my husband couldn't please me sexually but believe me, that's not it either. You do please me ALL the time. *(After a breath.)* It's standing behind you, that bothers me. That's where the pain comes, from behind you. *(To Truman.)* Steve enters a room, and I enter behind him and I watch them. *(To Steve.)* I watch people, watch you, and I can't tell you how that hurts my heart. I just can't tell you. It's the pain where you don't expect it. *(Getting to the core of it.)* They live a sickening shallow existence because they believe what their eyes tell them and they never trust what they cannot see. They cannot be patient, they cannot be silent and they can not hear the subtle beating of their own hearts.

You Could Die Laughing
Billy St. John

Comic

Lucinda (fifty to sixty)

> Lucinda, a has-been stand-up comedienne, has been invited by a mysterious TV producer to audition for a new series.

LUCINDA: You want to know about me? Sure, I'll tell you. Lucinda Tate's the name. My life is an open book. It's titled: "In the Garden of Love, I Keep Picking the Stinkweeds." I've had every kind of spouse: the louse, the grouse, the souse, and the mouse. The louse was my first husband, Irving. We had the ideal marriage — for about ten minutes. I should have realized something was wrong when he and my maid of honor both disappeared from the reception for over an hour, but I was young and naïve. It was two years before I came to realize that Irving was chasing anything in a skirt . . . and I had a closet full of slacks. I showed Irving the door; my mistake was letting husband number two, George, come through it — George, the grouse. He groused about everything — my cleaning, my washing, my ironing, my cooking . . . my cooking . . . my cooking . . . Hey, I never claimed to be Betty Crocker. Heck, I can't even keep up with Mrs. Paul. Eventually, I gave George some coupons for fast-food restaurants and sent him on his way. That brings us to husband number three, Benny the souse. Benny had a drinking problem. I don't joke about Benny because that kind of problem is no laughing matter. I just mention him to keep the record straight. I'm happy to say he later got help and is doing well. My fourth and latest husband Willard was a mouse. As in timid? How timid was he, you ask . . . Willard was so shy he blushed at the sight of a plucked chicken . . . so shy that at parties he'd stand very still in a corner and hope people would mistake him for a statue . . . so shy that he kept his socks on when he trimmed his toenails. As you can tell, I'm an out-there kind' a gal, so Willard and I were not what you'd call compatible. I was fire, he was ice, and whenever I got near him, he started to puddle. When he eventually asked me for a divorce, I had to agree it was a good idea. Actually, he didn't "ask" me, he left me a note in my shoe. We untied the knot and went our separate ways. So, Stanley, if you still want a date, look me up when we get back to the states. I'm in the Yellow Pages under "Desperate."

You Could Die Laughing
Billy St. John

Comic

Helena (thirties)

> Helena, a catty, sarcastic comedienne, has been invited to audition
> for a new TV series by a mysterious producer. Here, she is performing
> for the others who have also been invited.

HELENA: Nice characterization, Corky. Me, I don't do characters. I just
talk . . . about my views, my experiences, my life in general. Hey —
let's be specific — I usually talk about what it's like to be a single
woman in a couple-driven society. Actually, I don't mind being single all that much — it's my mother who takes another step closer to
Looneyville each time I pass another birthday unmarried. In my early
twenties, she introduced me to handsome, smart young men with
bright futures. Now she encourages me to walk down any dark alley
I come across in hopes I'll meet a street person who's not too picky.
For a while she called a different pizza place every night and had them
deliver a pizza to my house. She said if one of the delivery men and
I hit it off, at least I would marry a man who made sure I never go
hungry. She finally quit after I told her I had gained fifteen pounds,
and the only unattached delivery people I had met were a sixteen-
year-old boy named Ralph and a woman named Brenda. I'm still trying to work off those pepperonis which went right to my thighs.
Mom still hasn't given up, though. Every night she calls and asks me
the same question: "Darling, did you meet Mr. Wonderful today?"
"No, Mom, I met Mr. Super-ego, Mr. Mama's Boy, and a couple of
Mr. Potato Heads." She says that where men are concerned, my standards are too high. Well, I'm sorry, but I insist that any potential husband of mine must be able to read words with more than five letters,
eat soup without dribbling on himself, and be able to breathe without the help of a respirator. If those standards are too high, then Mom

will just have to deal with it. I'm happy to say that last week I met a single guy who met two out of the three criteria. Who knows? — if my luck continues to improve, I just might meet the man for me any day now.

A Young Housewife

Judy GeBauer

Dramatic

Daisy (early twenties)

> In a surreal soliloquy of passion and violence, a young farm wife tries
> to come to terms with having murdered a drifter. Aghast at what she
> has done, she is afraid to tell her hot-tempered husband. As she walks
> home from the deed in a panic, she tries to makes sense of what's
> happened. She is on a country lane that runs between an unused barn
> and her house.

DAISY: I'll tell
Daniel I'm worried. I'll
tell Daniel he
should find some
time to go down the
hill to the old barn. I'll
tell Daniel I think
something's amiss there. He'll tell
me I'm being a worrywart. He'll
ask me what I think is amiss. I'll
tell him I've seen something
moving around in that
old barn. He'll say it's just the
bell cow or something.

But what if he comes to look?
He'll see it. Oh,
he'll see it. He'll see,
he'll find it. I'll
say nothing. I'll
not mention it at all. He'll

come home for dinner and
I'll say nothing.
I am lonely, lonely.
And that's why.
And that's all of why.

But I'll have to
tell him because I
can't just ... pretend ... you can't
leave something dead in
an old barn and just
pretend it's not there.

He touched my hands.
Touched my hands with
his rough hands.

Kissed each finger.

How hot it's getting.
I must keep out of the sun.
I must somehow get home now.

He kissed each finger.
He kissed this little scar.
with his rough lips.
I shouldn't have let him.
I should not have let him start.
I should have set down that plate
and walked away.
Told him
to eat and be on his way.

I should not have stayed to watch him eat.

Because he spoke to me softly

and because he was tender
and so tired,
and because he was so hungry
and mostly he was so lonely.
And he was passing through is all,
just passing through.

He never meant it to happen. He
wasn't that sort. I didn't mean
it to happen. He put aside the
plate. I touched the plate and
he touched it, too, in the
same spot at the same time. His
fingers touched my fingers.

I could tell Daniel that much.
But how can I explain why that
bread knife is in his ribs?
I can't even explain that to my own self.
He didn't plan to touch me,
I know he didn't, anymore
than I planned him to. There
was no thought to it. It's how
you come together some way. No
rhyme or reason. His hand
touched my hand and we
came together some way.

But why did I let him?
What with Daniel and all,
why did I let him? Why
did I let him make me feel
that way?
Why did I put that knife in him?
If I could explain that,
then I know Daniel would understand.

I hurt him for some reason.
A kind of passion took hold of me
and it took me so fierce
I couldn't shake it. I couldn't
get free. I needed to slow it down,
I needed it to subside a little.
And so I hurt him. I only needed
it to stop, so much feeling at once,
It scared me, it was so strong in me.

I'd have liked to know his last name at least.